RESOURCE BOOKS FOR TEACHERS

series editor
ALAN MALEY

CULTURAL AWARENESS

Barry Tomalin &
Susan Stempleski

Oxford University Press

Oxford University Press
Walton Street, Oxford OX2 6DP

Oxford New York Toronto Madrid
Delhi Bombay Calcutta Madras Karachi
Kuala Lumpur Singapore Hong Kong Tokyo
Nairobi Dar es Salaam Cape Town
Melbourne Auckland

and associated companies in
Berlin Ibadan

Oxford and *Oxford English* are trade marks of
Oxford University Press

ISBN 0 19 437194 8

© Oxford University Press 1993

First published 1993
Second impression 1994

Set by Wyvern Typesetting, Bristol

Printed in Hong Kong

Acknowledgements

The publisher and author would like to thank the following for their kind permission to use articles, extracts, or adaptations from copyright material. There might be instances where we have been unable to trace or contact the copyright holder before our printing deadline. We apologize for this and if notified the publisher will be pleased to rectify any errors or omissions at the earliest opportunity.

Illustrations by OUP Technical Graphics Dept.

Studio Photography by Mark Mason

The publishers would like to thank the following for their kind permission to reproduce photographs:

James Davis Travel Photography
Mary Evans Picture Library
National Trust Photographic Library
Rex Features Ltd
The Wordsworth Trust
New York Convention and Visitors' Bureau
Oxford and County Newspapers.

Contents

The authors and series editor

Barry Tomalin is a writer, trainer, and broadcaster on educational matters, specializing in the use of educational technology, including video. He trained at International House in the UK, and has been a teacher trainer in Algeria, West Africa, and Paris. Since 1977 he has worked at BBC English in the BBC World Service and has lectured all over the world, training teachers in language teaching methodology, especially in the use of video. He is the author of numerous books and articles, including the self-study video course *Follow Me*, *Video in Action* (with Susan Stempleski), and *Video in the English Class*. His interest in the teaching of cultural awareness arises from his research into video and from working with different national groups in Europe, Latin America, the United States, and the Far East. He is married with one son.

Susan Stempleski has been involved in EFL/ESL since 1966. She has been a Fulbright lecturer in Bolivia, and a United States–Spain Joint Committee lecturer in Spain. As an Academic Specialist for the United States Information Agency, she has conducted teacher training and development programmes in Turkey, Burundi, Chile, Czechoslovakia, Ecuador, Greece, and South Africa. She is based in New York City, where, in addition to teaching at the Hunter College International English Language Institute of the City University of New York and at Teachers College, Columbia University, she is a freelance consultant and writer. Her numerous publications include *Video in Action* (with Barry Tomalin) and *Hello, America*.

Alan Maley worked for The British Council from 1962 to 1988, serving as English Language Officer in Yugoslavia, Ghana, Italy, France, and China, and as Regional Representative for The British Council in South India (Madras). From 1988 to 1993 he was Director-General of the Bell Educational Trust, Cambridge. He is currently Senior Fellow in the Department of English Language and Literature of the National University of Singapore. He has written *Literature*, in this series, *Beyond Words*, *Sounds Interesting*, *Sounds Intriguing*, *Words*, *Variations on a Theme*, and *Drama Techniques in Language Learning* (all with Alan Duff), *The Mind's Eye* (with Françoise Grellet and Alan Duff), and *Learning to Listen* and *Poem into Poem* (with Sandra Moulding). He is also Series Editor for the New Perspectives and Oxford Supplementary Skills series.

Foreword

In Classical–Humanist models of language education, culture (which usually meant high culture with a capital C) traditionally occupied a prominent position. More recent models have tended to stress the behavioural aspects of culture, and in particular its role in communication (and communication breakdown). Indeed, the concept of 'culture' has become something of a fashionable cliché in language-teaching circles in recent years.

This book strips away the layers of obfuscation which clichés invariably generate. It reminds us of *why* 'culture' is a valuable component of foreign-language programmes, and shows us *how* we might go about incorporating it into our teaching.

The title is not without significance. It remains doubtful whether culture, high or low, can really be taught, though generations of learners have been taught *about* culture. This book attempts to show that what we can do is to raise awareness of cultural factors. In so doing, we shall aim to sharpen observation, encourage critical thinking about cultural stereotypes, and develop tolerance. These are educational issues which reach out well beyond mere language teaching. Cultural awareness-raising is an aspect of values education. As such it offers a welcome opportunity for transcending the often narrow limits of language teaching.

The book might equally well have carried the title *Culture as a Language-Learning Resource*, for the activities, at the same time as raising cultural awareness, also offer a rich array of interesting and highly motivating language-learning resource material. The dual aims of the book are thus closely intertwined: to raise cultural awareness, and, in so doing, to promote language learning.

The authors adopt a common-sense, pragmatic approach, allowing the materials to speak for themselves. This will be welcome in a field notorious for obscurantism and vague, high-sounding terminology.

Perhaps the most valuable message of the book is that, while cultures may differ, people none the less share a common humanity.

Alan Maley

Introduction

Cultural awareness is the term we have used to describe
sensitivity to the impact of culturally-induced behaviour on
language use and communication. 'Cross-cultural awareness' in
this book covers British and American life and institutions,
beliefs, and values, as well as everyday attitudes and feelings
conveyed not only by language, but by paralinguistic features
such as dress, gesture, facial expression, stance, and movement.

In writing this book, we chose the term *cultural awareness*
because we felt it most successfully encompassed the three
qualities which the activities were designed to develop, namely:

– awareness of one's own culturally-induced behaviour;
– awareness of the culturally-induced behaviour of others;
– ability to explain one's own cultural standpoint.

Although cross-cultural interaction is one of the fastest-growing
areas of language study, the systematic study of cross-cultural
interaction may be new for many teachers. For this reason it is
important to explore a number of background questions which
teachers have asked.

Why is the study of cross-cultural interaction important?

A number of factors, both linguistic and socio-economic, have
raised the study of cross-cultural interaction to high international
profile in recent years. They are:

1 The rise in economic importance of the Pacific Rim countries

Countries such as Japan, Korea, Malaysia, Taiwan, and Thailand
have very different traditions and cultural behaviours from the
traditional ELT heartlands of Europe and North America. As
increasing numbers of students have travelled abroad to learn
English, there has been a re-evaluation of teaching content to
take account of the need to explore and explain cultural
differences in greater detail.

2 The influence of increased immigration on curricula

Teachers of English as a second or foreign language in English-speaking countries have long recognized the need to teach the way of life of the host country to immigrants. However, in recent years, a more open recognition of the need to understand the immigrant community's way of life has led to a more critical awareness of the host community's culture.

3 The study of pragmatics

Linguistic studies in the field of pragmatics (the ways in which language use is influenced by social context) have heightened awareness of the degree to which cross-cultural communication is affected by culturally-related factors. Such factors include people's expectations regarding the appropriate level of formality and degree of politeness in discourse.

4 The study of non-verbal aspects of communication

Of crucial importance has been the work on non-verbal aspects of communication such as gesture, posture, and facial expression. Studies have shown these non-verbal elements to be the most culturally-influenced part of behaviour.

All these different factors are reflected in the activities in this book.

What culture do we teach?

The study of British and American/Canadian life and institutions has been a traditional part of school curricula in Europe and North America. Sometimes it has taken the form of special courses, such as *Civilisation* in France, *Landeskunde* in Germany, and *Civiltà* in Italy. These courses emphasize the 'big C' elements of British and American culture—history, geography, institutions, literature, art, and music—and the way of life.

We have to recognize that the subject itself has broadened as a result of the influences described above. 'Big C' ('achievement culture') remains as it was, but 'little c' ('behaviour culture') has been broadened to include culturally-influenced beliefs and perceptions, especially as expressed through language, but also through cultural behaviours that affect acceptability in the host community. Gail Robinson (1985), an American researcher in the area of cross-cultural education, reports that when teachers are asked, 'What does culture mean to you?', the most common responses fall into three interrelated categories: products, ideas, and behaviours. The broadening of 'little c' (behaviour culture) can be expressed through the following diagram.

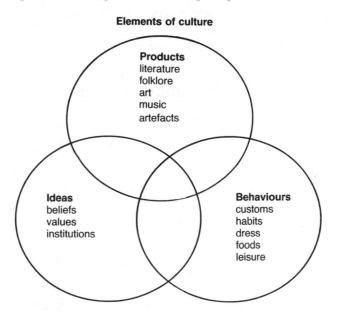

Elements of culture

Products
literature
folklore
art
music
artefacts

Ideas
beliefs
values
institutions

Behaviours
customs
habits
dress
foods
leisure

'Big C' culture has benefited from a clearly identified curriculum of topics to be covered, and textbooks which deal with them. The culturally-influenced behaviours which constitute 'little c' culture have tended to be treated in an anecdotal, peripheral, or supplementary way, depending on the interest and awareness of teachers and students. In our view, the study of culturally-influenced behaviour should arise out of the language material being studied, but should nevertheless be clearly identified and systematically treated as a regular feature of the language lesson.

It is difficult to identify a detailed syllabus for the study of culturally-influenced behaviour, although the revised Council of Europe Waystage 90 and Threshold 90 specifications for English do include a section on socio-economic competence. In *Teaching Culture*, Ned Seelye (1988) provides a framework for facilitating the development of cross-cultural communication skills. The following goals are a modification of his 'seven goals of cultural instruction':

1 To help students to develop an understanding of the fact that all people exhibit culturally-conditioned behaviours.

2 To help students to develop an understanding that social variables such as age, sex, social class, and place of residence influence the ways in which people speak and behave.

3 To help students to become more aware of conventional behaviour in common situations in the target culture.

4 To help students to increase their awareness of the cultural connotations of words and phrases in the target language.

5 To help students to develop the ability to evaluate and refine generalizations about the target culture, in terms of supporting evidence.

6 To help students to develop the necessary skills to locate and organize information about the target culture.

7 To stimulate students' intellectual curiosity about the target culture, and to encourage empathy towards its people.

We recommend that you keep these 'seven goals of cultural instruction' in mind as you do your lesson planning, and that you incorporate them into the following practical teaching principles:

1 Access the culture through the language being taught.

2 Make the study of cultural behaviours an integral part of each lesson.

3 Aim for students to achieve the socio-economic competence which they feel they need.

4 Aim for all levels to achieve cross-cultural understanding— awareness of their own culture, as well as that of the target language.

5 Recognize that not all teaching about culture implies behaviour change, but merely an awareness and tolerance of the cultural influences affecting one's own and others' behaviour.

What materials and what approach?

A wide range of materials is available for the study of culturally-influenced behaviour. These include course textbooks, audio-cassettes (ELT-based and others), radio broadcasts, TV broadcasts, specialist British and American textbooks and readers, videos, cuttings from newspapers and magazines, and all kinds of realia from Underground tickets to replicas of the Statue of Liberty or Big Ben!

These are the kinds of materials which you and your students can use to research cultural information. However, effective use of such materials requires careful planning by the teacher. Little benefit will result from merely displaying a cultural document or artefact in class. Students need to be trained to extract appropriate information from the material.

We strongly advocate a task-oriented approach towards teaching culture. The approach is characterized by co-operative learning tasks in which students

– work together in pairs or small groups to gather precise segments of information;
– share and discuss what they have discovered, in order to form a more complete picture;
– interpret the information within the context of the target culture and in comparison with their own culture(s).

In our own teaching we have found that, when students have understood the language being used in a situation and then go on to gain an understanding of the cultural factors at work, this is for them one of the most absorbing and exciting parts of any language lesson. Studying culture with a task-oriented and co-operative learning approach adds a new dimension of achievement and understanding for the students—and for us as teachers!

How to use this book

Who the book is for

This book is for language teachers who are using or want to use
activities to increase cultural *awareness* among their students and
to promote cross-cultural *interaction* in the classroom. It contains
75 activities for use with students at any level of language ability,
from elementary to advanced. The activities are described in the
context of teaching English as a second or foreign language.
However, with modification, they can be used for teaching any
foreign or second language. We are conscious that many of the
activities can also be adapted for use in social studies classes or
cross-cultural training courses in which there is no second- or
foreign-language teaching component.

How the book is organized

The activities are divided into seven sections, dealing with
cognitive as well as affective aspects of cultural awareness. The
activities within each section are arranged in alphabetical order.
You may find it useful to consult the introduction to each of the
seven sections for more specific information on the pedagogical
aim of each section.

Recognizing cultural images and symbols

This section introduces students to the concept of culture, and
encourages them to discuss it from the start. It contains activities
designed to help students to familiarize themselves with popular
images and symbols, expressed in personalities, architectural
features, landscape, and song.

Working with cultural products

This section contains activities based on realia, using postcards,
stamps, newspapers, and radio broadcasts—all readily available
to teachers overseas.

3 Examining patterns of everyday life

This section contains activities which focus on the lifestyles of people in English-speaking cultures, and on what people in these cultures usually do in common situations (for example, employment, dating, shopping) that are part of normal everyday experience.

4 Examining cultural behaviour

This section contains information-oriented activities designed to raise awareness of culturally-appropriate behaviour in English-speaking countries, as well as activities involving experiential learning and awareness of the students' own culturally-influenced behaviour.

5 Examining patterns of communication

This section contains activities designed to increase awareness of the expectations of native speakers about verbal and non-verbal communication in English.

6 Exploring values and attitudes

This section contains activities designed to increase awareness of the students' own culturally-influenced values, as well as the cultural values and attitudes of people in English-speaking cultures.

7 Exploring and extending cultural experiences

This section contains activities that allow the students to explore and to share their own experiences of the target culture.

All of the activities are cross-referenced in the two Indexes at the back of the book.

The indexes

The first index, the Index of skills, provides a brief overview of the language skills (discussion, listening, note-taking, oral composition, etc.) practised in the various activities. The second index, the Index of structures, groups the activities according to the various grammatical structures that are practised.

The activities

Each activity offers you the following information: the cross-cultural aim of the activity, the materials needed, the level at which the activity can be used, how long the activity will take to complete, what preparation is needed, and step-by-step directions for carrying out the activity in class. Where appropriate, variations of the activity have been included.

Bibliography

We have also included a bibliography of reference materials on the theory of cross-cultural instruction and source materials which can help you to become more aware of cultural issues.

This is all you need to know to go straight to the activities. Enjoy the book!

1 Recognizing cultural images and symbols

When we live in a particular country, we automatically become exposed and accustomed to a range of images and symbols embedded in songs and pictures, places, and customs. These images and symbols include famous people in the culture, and architectural and landscape features such as the White House in Washington and the white cliffs of Dover. Familiarity with these images helps students to feel more confident and to become more fluent.

The aim of the activities in this section is to familiarize students with popular images and symbols in the target culture. A secondary aim is to help students to identify and compare the images and symbols in British and American culture, and then to contrast these with the images and symbols in their own. 'Culture match' (1.4) and 'Odd one out' (1.8) focus on comparisons of cultural features. 'Guess who? Guess what?' (1.7), 'Postcard match' (1.9), 'Rogues' gallery' (1.10), and 'Where in the world?' (1.12) focus on places and people associated with the culture. Much of what the students learn in other activities in this section may be developed into a 'Culture wallchart' project.

Words and phrases also help to identify a culture. In 'Word chase' (1.13) students use dictionaries to find key word fields, such as words connected with dwellings. At the same time, they learn where the words have come from and how they are used in another culture. 'Ten-word story' (1.11) is an oral composition activity designed to revise key words and phrases. At a deeper level, 'Exploring song lyrics' (1.6) allows the learner to explore the cultural references in popular songs.

One area of a culture often ignored is that of its sounds. A cultural milieu can be identified by the sounds of people, cars, artefacts, and even the countryside. Enabling students to recognize these signals in 'Background noise' (1.2) can help to make listening more focused and to improve their listening comprehension.

Two of the activities in this section deal with ways of approaching culture: 'All about culture' (1.1) encourages students to explore the concept of culture itself, and 'Brainstorming' (1.3) provides a way for you, the teacher, to find out what the students know about a subject before presenting it in class.

Materials for these activities can be found in newspapers and magazines from Britain and America, and also in local magazines and newspapers.

1.1 All about culture

AIM
To increase awareness of the different meanings which people ascribe to the word 'culture', and the way the term is used to indicate that people are different from one another; to stimulate discussion about one's own culture and how it differs from others

MATERIALS
No special materials are needed

LEVEL
Intermediate and above

TIME
60 minutes

PREPARATION
No special preparation is needed.

IN CLASS
1 Explain to the class that there are many definitions of the word 'culture', and that they are going to carry out an activity to find out what the members of the class think of when the word 'culture' is mentioned.

2 Ask the class to name as many cultural groups as they can. As the students call them out, write them up on the board.

3 When you have 15–20 names of cultural groups, divide the class into groups of three or four. Explain that each group is to work together to draw up a list of characteristics that make each of the cultural groups different from all the others. Allow ten minutes for the groups to make up their lists. Here is a sample of the kind of list they might produce:

language	religion	music
race	national origin	geography
architecture	customs	arts and crafts
clothing	physical features	food

4 Ask a volunteer from each group to read out their list, while you write up the characteristics.

5 When the students have reached the end of their lists, ask them which characteristics apply to all of the cultural groups they mentioned. For example, can all the groups be identified by different languages or by different religions? The students will realize that very few, if any, of the characteristics apply to all the groups.

6 Conduct a whole-class discussion on the basis of the following questions:
– *Why is it difficult to define the word 'culture'?*
– *Why do people identify with cultures and cultural groups?*

VARIATION 1

As an extension to this activity, ask the following questions:
– *Is anyone in the class a member of any of the groups mentioned? If so, which group? If not, with which cultural groups do you identify?*
– *How do you feel about the terms 'culture' and 'cultural group'? If you like the term, why? If not, why not?*
– *What other term would you prefer (national group, ethnic group, or no term at all)? Why?*
  etc.

VARIATION 2

Another variation, instead of working through Step 3 above, is to ask the students to brainstorm and draw up a list of cultural images and symbols they associate with three or four of the cultural groups identified in Step 2. For example, a list of symbols relating to US culture might include: baseball, the Statue of Liberty, the American flag, hot dogs, Elvis Presley, cowboys, the White House, etc.

REMARKS

Answers in the discussion stage (Step 6) will vary. The important points to bring out are:
a. The characteristics which people use to name cultural differences cannot be applied universally.
b. People identify cultures and cultural groups as a way of indicating that the groups are different from one another. In the context of this activity, it does not matter whether the students formulate a specific definition of the term 'culture'. What matters is the way the term is used to indicate human differences.

Acknowledgement
This activity is an adaptation of 'What is culture?' in G. Smith and G. Otero, *Teaching About Cultural Awareness* (Denver, Col.: Center for Teaching International Relations, 1977; revised 1988).

1.2 Background noise

AIM

To help students to tune in to a cultural context as an introduction to listening comprehension

MATERIALS

Listening and viewing material with sound effects typical of the culture being studied

LEVEL

Elementary and above

TIME

10 minutes

PREPARATION

1 Select a video or audio sequence in which some dialogue is preceded by sound effects of, for example, a London bus, a New York subway, loudspeaker announcements, etc. (This activity can lead into a longer comprehension activity.)

2 Set up the tape recorder or VCR and monitor in the classroom.

IN CLASS

1 Write the following pairs of words and phrases on the board:

indoors	*outdoors*
day	*night*
machines	*people*
natural	*electronic*
two people	*a number of people*

2 Tell the students that they are going to hear some sounds, and that they are to think about what the sounds mean and where the scene takes place. Using the words on the board, they try to guess:
– where it is
– what time of day it is
– whether they can hear sounds of people or machines
– whether they can hear natural sounds (like the wind) or electronic sounds (such as car horns)
– whether there are any people and, if so, how many.

3 Play the sequence without the picture (with sound only), and stop it before the dialogue begins.

4 The students decide among themselves:
– where the sequence takes place
– what the situation is
– what is happening.

5 Next, play the sequence with the picture on and with the dialogue, so that the students can check their answers.

6 The sequence can then be used to study the language content.

1.3 Brainstorming

AIM   **Preparation for a 'Life and institutions' presentation**

MATERIALS   **No special materials are needed**

LEVEL   **Intermediate and above**

TIME   **10 minutes**

PREPARATION   1 To do a 'Life and institutions' presentation, it is important to find out what the students already know about the topic, and to get them involved from the start. The simplest way of doing this is to brainstorm.

2 Choose the topic for presentation (for example, 'The White House').

IN CLASS   1 Write the topic in a circle in the centre of the board.

2 Ask the class to call out any words or phrases they know associated with the topic. They may volunteer things like 'the Oval Office', 'Jackie Kennedy', 'where the President of the United States lives', 'Washington', 'Congress', etc.

3 Write up each word or phrase, as in the spidergram below.

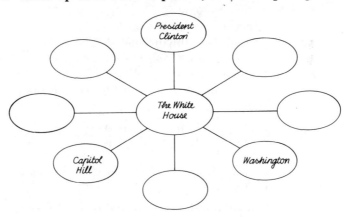

4 Make sure that everybody in the class understands all the words and phrases.

5 Draw a line with a question mark on it between words or phrases that seem to contradict each other. For example:

White House _____?_____ *Congress*

6 Tell the students to work in pairs to ask and answer questions around the contradictions. For example:
A *Does Congress meet in the White House?*
B *No, it doesn't. It meets on Capitol Hill.*

7 When you have gathered as much information as the students know, do your 'Life and institutions' presentation, making sure to incorporate all the points raised by the class.

1.4 Culture match

AIM

To increase awareness of symbols and events in Anglo-American culture; to increase awareness of symbols and events in the culture(s) represented by the class

MATERIALS

Index cards

LEVEL

Intermediate and above

TIME

30 minutes

PREPARATION

1 Prepare a list of pairs of corresponding American/British cultural items. For example:
- *Congress/Parliament*
- *President/Prime Minister*
- *baseball/soccer*
- *White House/10 Downing Street*
- *Bill of Rights/Magna Carta*
- *Stars and Stripes/Union Jack*
- *1766 (Declaration of Independence)/1688 (The Glorious Revolution)*
- *Franklin D. Roosevelt/Winston Churchill*

2 Make sure you have as many items as there are students in the class. Write one item on every index card. Prepare enough cards to give one to each student.

IN CLASS

1 Give a card to each student. Tell the students to circulate and find a student with an item that matches theirs. When the students find their cultural match, they write their pair of items on the board.

2 When all the students have found their match, each pair reports to the class what their items are, and which one refers to Britain, and which to the US. They tell the class all they know about their topics. If a pair has difficulty with information about their topic, you or the other students can act as informants.

3 The students then work in groups to discuss the list of items on the board. For each pair of items, they provide the equivalent event, person, or institution from their own culture, and if necessary, give some background information to you and the rest of the class.

Acknowledgement
This activity is an adaptation of one described in an article by
Luke Prodromou in the June 1992 issue of *Practical English
Teaching*.

1.5 Culture wallchart

AIM

**To encourage the spirit of investigation; to deepen knowledge
of a particular topic**

MATERIALS

**Pictures/drawings/newspaper articles/photographs/several large
sheets of white paper, coloured pens, and paste**

LEVEL

Elementary and above

TIME

180 minutes (over several class sessions)

PREPARATION

1 Collect a number of magazines and papers with articles or
pictures about the topic.

2 Clear a space on the classroom wall and bring to class a few
large sheets of coloured paper to use for displaying the
presentation, as well as coloured pens or felt-tips and paste.

IN CLASS

Day 1

1 Tell the students that they are going to create a wallchart
about a particular topic, for example, the work of Congress,
Yellowstone National Park, or the Lake District.

2 The class divide the topic into four to six sub-topics. Each
sub-topic becomes the subject of one panel of the presentation.

3 Divide the class into groups of four or five, and allocate one
sub-topic to each group.

4 Distribute the articles and pictures you have collected, giving
each group material relevant to its sub-topic.

5 The groups study the material and plan their presentation
sheet.

6 Encourage the groups at the end of the class to look for
additional information, either by interviewing someone, or by
collecting more pictures, postcards, etc. Set a date for completion
of this phase of the project.

Day 2

At the end of the research period, the learners create their sub-
topic presentation sheets, using the pens, paper, and paste
provided.

SAMPLE WALLCHART

William Wordsworth
1770 – 1850

William Wordsworth was a famous British poet, who lived in the Lake District. He was born in this house in Cockermouth. But he wrote a lot of his poems at Dove Cottage in Grasmere (a lake).

Wordsworth House

A very popular poem is "Daffodils". It begins like this.

"I wandered, lonely as a cloud
That floats on high o'er
vales and hills
And all at once I saw a crowd
A host of golden daffodils."

Here is a garden of daffodils he planted for his daughter, Dora. The garden's name is Dora's field.

Dove Cottage

Dora's Field, Rydal

Day 3

1 Each group presents its sub-topic to the rest of the class.

2 Finally, the panels are mounted on the classroom wall as a permanent exhibition.

REMARKS

1 This activity is an excellent way of giving a class the feelings of hands-on involvement with a cultural feature, even if they are unable to experience it at first hand.

2 In some cases the presentation can be put on video and made available for other classes studying the same topic.

3 This activity can be the basis for exploration of a topic, or a way of consolidating work on a topic already studied.

Contents of a sample presentation

- Pictures of the Lake District
- List of main places to visit (Ullswater, Derwentwater, Wordsworth's cottage, Skiddaw, etc.)
- Map showing where to go
- Seven-line history of the Lake District
- Eye-witness account (interview with someone who has visited)
- Sports and leisure in the Lake District (walking, water skiing, sailing)
- Writers in the Lake District (Wordsworth, Coleridge, Southey)
- Ecology of the Lake District (birds, flowers, and trees identified with the Lake District)

1.6 Exploring song lyrics

AIM

To increase awareness of the cultural images and references used in pop songs and music videos

MATERIALS

Pre-recorded songs on audio-cassette, CD, or video; a task sheet for each student

LEVEL

Intermediate and above

TIME

60 minutes

PREPARATION

1 Choose a song with cultural references. We recommend the following criteria for choosing a song which will work well in class:

a. Choose a song that tells a story, and that is not too long.

b. Make sure the words are distinguishable.

c. Choose a song with a clear melodic line distinguishing between verse and chorus.

d. If possible, choose songs that have the lyrics printed on the cassette or CD inlay.

e. Choose songs which you yourself enjoy!

2 Make sure you have enough copies of the task sheet below and the song lyrics, to give one to each student.

3 Set up the cassette/CD player or the video recorder.

IN CLASS

Tell the students that you are going to play a song on cassette/CD. They are going to explore the song in four stages, listening to it for mood, lyrics, meaning, and cultural references.

Stage 1

1 Play the song.

2 Ask the students to choose one word that they think describes the mood of the song. For example, *sad, happy, optimistic, bitter,* etc.

3 Ask the students to write down the word they choose, and then work in pairs to compare their words.

4 Ask the pairs to call out their words and to say why they chose those moods.

5 Play the song again. At the end, each student completes the sentence: *This song is about...*

6 Again, ask the students to explain why they wrote what they wrote.

Stage 2

1 Tell the class you are going to play the song line by line. They are to listen and call out the words they hear.

2 Play the first line, then pause the cassette/CD player.

3 The students call out words and phrases, while you write them on the board, until the whole song is complete.

4 Explain the meaning of any words which the class do not understand.

Stage 3

1 Divide the class into groups of three or four.

2 The groups look back at their sentences beginning *This song is about...* and, in the light of the lyrics, discuss the overall meaning of the song, the singer's attitude, etc.

Stage 4

1 Ask the students to remain in their groups, and distribute the task sheets you have prepared.

IN CLASS

1 Hold up a photograph of a person, with the picture facing you.

2 Tell the students which country the person comes from.

3 The class then ask you questions to try and identify the person. You may only answer *Yes* or *No*.

4 The class ask questions such as:
Is it a man or a woman?
Is he/she alive?
Is he/she a Prince/Princess?

5 When the class have guessed who the first person is, let a student come up to the front of the class, choose a different picture, and take your place.

VARIATION

1 Hold up a picture of an object or cultural feature.

2 The class describe the picture. They might say, for instance: *The picture shows milk bottles on a doorstep.*

3 The students then try to explain or guess the cultural connection, for example: *In Britain, milk is delivered to people every day in glass bottles.*

1.8 Odd one out

AIM

To recognize cultural and geographical features

MATERIALS

Newspapers/postcards/photographs/pictures

LEVEL

Elementary and above

TIME

10 minutes

PREPARATION

Assemble several sets of five newspaper mastheads, photographs, or names of games, places, etc. and mount them on cards. For example:
1 Queen Elizabeth II, Prince Philip, Prince Charles, Princess Anne, President Clinton (odd one out—US president)
2 *New York Times, Herald Tribune, Washington Post, Chicago Herald, The Guardian* (odd one out—British newspaper)
3 Baseball, softball, American football, ice hockey, soccer (odd one out—British national sport)
Four of the cards should represent one particular culture or country. The fifth should be of a different culture or country. Prepare enough sets for the class to work in groups with one set each.

IN CLASS

1 Divide the class into groups of three to five students.

2 Give each group a set of pictures. One set might consist, for example, of four pictures of London and one of Shanghai.

3 The students try to identify each place, and then find the odd one out.

4 When they have all finished, the groups describe their pictures or cards to the class, and say why one is the odd one out.

1.9 Postcard match

AIM

Understanding written messages; recognizing geographical features; information gathering

MATERIALS

Postcards and index cards

LEVEL

Lower-intermediate and above

TIME

30 minutes

PREPARATION

1 Assemble enough postcards of different places for half the class.

2 On the same number of index cards, write a message to go with each card. Decide what you want the task to be, and write that on the card as well. For example, to go with a postcard of Central Park in New York you might write:

We stayed right in the centre, near a beautiful park. I can't remember its name. Do you recognize it?

IN CLASS

1 Tell the students that half of them will get a postcard, and the other half will get an index card with a message and a task on it. The student with the message has to find the person with the matching postcard. Together they will complete the task.

2 Hand out the postcards and index cards at random.

3 Make sure everyone understands what countries the cards come from and what the messages mean.

4 The students then mingle to look for their match. When they find it, the students with the index cards look at the postcards and try to guess the answers.

5 The pairs then read out their message, show their card, and tell the class the answer to the question or puzzle.

6 Take in the postcards and index cards, shuffle them, and hand them out again, making sure that the students who had a postcard the first time get an index card this time. This way, everyone gets a chance to ask questions and do the task.

VARIATION 1

1 Divide the class into pairs and give each pair a postcard (which the students must not write on—it will be needed for other classes) and a piece of paper. Each pair writes on the piece of paper, describing the card, then passes both on to another pair.

2 The new pairs read the description and comment on whether the message evokes/describes the card.

VARIATION 2

1 Give each pair a postcard and ask them to react to it as themselves. For example, if you give out a card of a pebble beach, students might write *I don't understand anyone going to a beach like that. It looks very uncomfortable. Here the beaches are sandy.*

REMARKS

To build up a stock of cards, make sure you never let a student go abroad on holiday without sending you one!

1.10 Rogues' gallery

AIM

To identify well-known historical or present-day personalities from the target culture

MATERIALS

Photographs, pictures, questionnaires, four large sheets of white paper, and paste

LEVEL

Lower-intermediate

TIME

180 minutes (over three class sessions)

PREPARATION

1 Make enough copies of the 'Rogues' gallery' questionnaire opposite to give one to each student in the class.

2 Take four large sheets of white paper and some paste to class.

IN CLASS

Day 1

1 Distribute the questionnaire.

2 Explain the task. Each student is to interview someone in the class to try and get answers to the questions on the questionnaire.

3 If the students are unable to complete the questionnaire in class, they can take it home and put the questions to someone outside the class.

4 For the next class, the students bring back their completed questionnaires.

Day 2

1 Go through the questionnaire, question by question, with the class.

2 As the class call out names, ask one student to list them on the board and put a tick alongside the names each time the same name is mentioned.

3 At the end of the session, count up the names with the largest number of ticks. These personalities will be considered 'the most'. There should be twelve names.

4 Divide the class into four groups, and tell them that for the next session each group is to find and bring photographs or pictures of three of the famous people. Assign three names to each group.

Day 3

1 The groups show you the photos and pictures they have collected.

2 They then use the sheets of paper to mount the pictures on a 'Rogues' gallery' poster. They give each picture a name and title, and then put the poster up on the wall for reference.

QUESTIONNAIRE

1 Who is the most famous monarch/President? _____

2 Who is the most famous politician? _____

3 Who is the most famous General? _____

4 Who is the most famous poet? _____

5 Who is the most important writer? _____

6 Who is the most famous actor/actress? _____

7 Who is the most famous criminal? _____

8 Who is the most famous sports person? _____

9 Who is the most famous scientist/inventor? _____

10 Who is the most famous artist? _____

11 Who is the most important historical figure? _____

12 Who is the most famous singer? _____

All the above questions can refer to people alive or dead.

VARIATION 1

This activity can also be done using famous people and personalities from the students' own culture(s). Comparison of the results can be most interesting.

VARIATION 2

At higher language levels, comparisons can be made, not just of the personalities, but also of the values implicit in the students' choices. For example, in one country, the most important historical/cult figure might be a military general, in another it might be a great religious leader or a saint. This kind of comparison will need very careful handling, however, as it may give rise to strong feelings.

REMARKS

A 'Rogues' gallery' is the popular name for any poster with photographs of well-known people (even from one's own school!). The name is derived from the tradition of putting up notices showing the names and faces of criminals wanted by the police.

1.11 Ten-word story

AIM Revision and composition; recycling culture-related vocabulary

MATERIALS No special materials are needed

LEVEL Intermediate and above

TIME 20 minutes

PREPARATION Select ten culture-related words that you would like to revise. For example:

cheerful

win *successful*

competitive *black*

homeless

Oscar

mother

struggle

white

IN CLASS

1 Write the ten words on the board, or elicit them from the students.

2 Make sure that the class understand each word.

3 Tell the class they are to make up a story, using the ten words. (Whoever begins has ten words to choose from. Whoever ends has only one. The students can change the form of the word, or make it plural, etc.)

4 One student begins to tell the story and stops at the end of the sentence in which the first of the ten words is introduced. As each word is used, it should be ticked off on the board.

5 Next, a second student continues the story and stops when another of the words is introduced.

6 When the story is complete and all the words have been ticked, a new story can be made up, using the same set of words. This may be necessary in a large class, in order to give everyone a chance to speak.

7 As the students tell the story, check to make sure that the words are being used in appropriate cultural contexts, and with the correct connotations.

VARIATION

1 The activity can be extended by asking the class to vote for the 'best' story, and asking a student to come to the blackboard to reconstruct it with the help of the class.

2 At the end of the story, the class correct any errors.

3 Finally, the class copy down the story, as a record of how the ten words or expressions can be used, and in what contexts.

1.12 Where in the world...?

AIM	**To introduce a famous city or other place in the target culture; to stimulate discussion; to practise asking and answering *wh*-questions; to introduce and review vocabulary; to practise writing descriptions of places**
MATERIALS	**Slides of monuments and street scenes in the target culture**
LEVEL	**Intermediate and above**
TIME	**60 minutes**
PREPARATION	**1** Make a collection of 10–20 slides of monuments, street scenes, etc. in a well-known city or some other easily identifiable place in the target culture. (Some tourist shops sell sets of slides of particular cities, sights, and scenes.) For a slide sequence about New York, you might select slides showing the following:

– *World Trade Center*
– *East River skyline*
– *Statue of Liberty*
– *Brooklyn Bridge*

2 Set up the slide projector and screen in the classroom.

IN CLASS

1 Write the following questions on the board:
– *Where do you think the pictures were taken?*
– *Which of the places or buildings have you seen before? Where?*
– *Can you name some of the things you see in the pictures? Which things?*

2 Tell the class that you are going to show them some slides. Explain that you will show the sequence of slides twice. During the first viewing, they are to look at the slides and think about the questions on the board. During the second viewing, you will pause after each slide to allow students to make notes.

3 Show the slides, but do not make any commentary on them.

4 Show the slides a second time. After you show each one, pause long enough for the students to write down their answers to the questions.

5 Next, divide the class into groups of three or four. Each group discusses and compares their answers.

6 Show the slides a third time and ask for volunteers to answer questions about each picture as it is shown. For example, with a slide of the Statue of Liberty, you might ask questions such as:
– *What do you see in the picture?*
– *What does she represent?*
– *Can anyone tell the class a story about the Statue of Liberty?*

VARIATION 1

Students can be asked to make an oral summary (with or without consulting their notes) of the things they have seen in the slides and the characteristics of the places they show.

VARIATION 2

Students can be asked to choose one slide that interests them and to write a description of it, perhaps for homework.

VARIATION 3

Students can choose two different slides to compare and contrast, either orally or in writing.

Acknowledgement
This activity was developed by Dimas A. González in a workshop at Teachers College, Columbia University.

1.13 Word chase

AIM	**To extend vocabulary and to develop research skills**
MATERIALS	**No special materials are needed**
LEVEL	**Lower-intermediate and above**
TIME	**20 minutes**

PREPARATION

1 Make sure that you have in the classroom an English dictionary and a bilingual learners' dictionary. There are several appropriate English dictionaries, for example, the *Oxford Students'* and the *Oxford Advanced Learners' Dictionary* for British English, and the *Oxford ESL Dictionary for Students of American English* for American English.

IN CLASS

1 Choose a word or phrase that has cultural connotations, for example: *Oxon.*

2 The class look up the word in the dictionary and find its meaning.

> **Oxon** / ˈɒksn/ *abbr* 1(esp in addresses) Oxfordshire (Latin *Oxonia*). 2 (esp in degree titles) of Oxford University (Latin *Oxoniensis*): *Ann Hunter MA (Oxon)*. Cf CANTAB.

3 Work with the class to find some more words associated with it. For example:

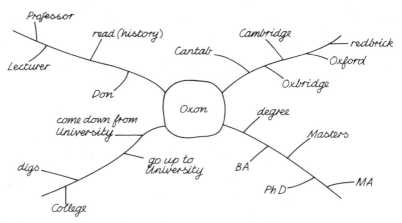

4 Divide the class into groups: one for each association in the spidergram. Allocate one word to each group and ask them to find out the meaning of that word.

5 At the end of the activity, ask the students to give feedback on the meaning of the words they looked up.

6 As a follow-up, the students write a paragraph about the topic, to include the information they have learned.

When the class has become more experienced at 'word-chasing', they can bring to class words or phrases they have seen, heard, or read—on TV or at the cinema, on the radio, in books and newspapers, or on posters and T-shirts.

1.14 Words and images

AIM

To increase awareness of the different images associated with some common words in British/American culture

MATERIALS

Magazine/newspaper pictures or photographic slides

LEVEL

Elementary and above

TIME

120 minutes (over two class sessions)

PREPARATION

1 Assemble a selection of 10–15 magazine/newspaper pictures or photographic slides illustrating a wide variety of British/American dwellings. For example, apartment blocks, brownstone houses, ranch houses, mobile homes, houseboats, semi-detached houses, cottages, terraced houses, bungalows, etc.

2 If you are going to use slides, set up the slide projector and screen in the classroom.

IN CLASS

Day 1

1 Write the word *home* on the board. Tell the students that you are going to show them some examples of what British/American speakers of English may mean when they use the word *home*.

2 Show each photograph/slide and name the kind of dwelling; say, for example: *This is an apartment block*.

3 Next, write the following words on the board:

man	*bread*	*woman*	*school*	*car*
church	*street*	*hat*	*room*	*office*
bag	*bed*	*shirt*	*ball*	*chair*
door	*table*	*book*	*party*	*room*

4 Explain to the students that, like the word *home*, the words in the list can mean many different things in the UK or the US.

5 For homework, ask the students each to select a word that interests them and to collect visual examples of their chosen word from British/American newspapers or magazines. Tell the

students that they should be prepared to show their collections to the class and say a brief sentence about each picture.

Day 2

6 In the next class period, students take turns to present their collections to the class.

REMARKS

The ability to visualize culturally appropriate images is essential to cross-cultural understanding. This seemingly simple activity encourages students to go beyond the dictionary and gain a perspective on the 'authentic' ways that concepts such as *man* or *bag* can be encountered and interpreted in the target culture.

Photocopiable © Oxford University Press

2 Working with cultural products

Every teacher is familiar with the concept of realia—physical objects such as postcards, photographs, images, and symbols associated with the target culture. Images and symbols may be found in song lyrics, idioms, and certain words and expressions. These items are not just useful as language-teaching material. Familiarity with them offers learners a cultural currency which helps them to feel more confident and to sound more fluent in the target culture.

The activities in this section are largely based on realia: souvenirs, cartoons, travelogues, money, photographs, newspapers, news on radio and TV, and stamps. These are obtainable relatively easily by overseas teachers, and they have the all-important function of bringing the world of the target culture into the classroom. Furthermore, it is extremely useful for classroom communication for the students to have actual physical objects in their hands to work with.

The aim of working with cultural products is to help students to build up language fluency by using authentic material from the target culture and to allow them, by observing and describing the realia, to compare these objects with others in their own cultures. An important aspect of these activities is their focus on a language skill: oral composition in 'Culture composition' (2.3), writing skills in 'Radio news role-plays' (2.10), and reading skills in 'Front-page features' (2.5) and 'Headlines' (2.6).

A key element of all the activities is to allow scope for personal involvement and the opportunity to express a personal response. In 'Stamp detectives' (2.12), students are asked to say what the images on postage stamps reveal to them about another culture. 'Poems' (2.9) and 'Today's TV schedule' (2.13) likewise provide the opportunity for new insights. In 'Among my souvenirs' (2.1), students are encouraged to bring to class objects, pictures, and posters to help to create a more authentic cultural environment. This is especially suitable for primary and lower-secondary students.

Teachers who have no opportunity to visit Britain or America need not feel discouraged about using this section. Cultural products are available everywhere—on T-shirts, in newspapers, in travel posters, and in materials available from cultural missions and expatriate workers.

2.1 Among my souvenirs

AIM

To create a mini-environment representative of the target culture; to find information about famous places and monuments; to extend vocabulary

MATERIALS

Postcards, souvenir objects (statuettes, knick-knacks, etc.), and one or two large sheets of white paper

LEVEL

Elementary

TIME

20 minutes

PREPARATION

Ask the students to bring to the class any objects, pictures, postcards, or souvenirs they may have from the target-culture country.

IN CLASS

1 Ask the students to arrange the objects on a table, and to put up the photographs and postcards on posters on the wall. Leave the objects in place for several class periods.

2 Ask the students to identify each of the items in English. As they do, write them up on the board.

3 Explain to the class, or get the students themselves to explain, what each of the items represents. For example: *This is the Statue of Liberty. It's in New York.*

4 Classes beyond elementary level will also be able to tell you where they or their family obtained the souvenirs, how old they are, and what they represent.

5 In a follow-up class, get the students to go through the items again, to practise asking questions such as:
– *What's this?*
– *Where does it come from?*
– *Who does it belong to?*
    etc.

REMARKS   Try to keep a semi-permanent collection of souvenirs and update it from time to time.

2.2. Cartoon categories

AIM   **To increase awareness of the subject matter of British and/or American cartoons; to compare British and/or American cartoons with cartoons in the students' own culture(s)**

MATERIALS   **Cartoons from British and/or American newspapers and magazines**

LEVEL   **Advanced**

TIME   **30 minutes**

PREPARATION   Select 15–20 cartoons from British and/or American newspapers and magazines. Make sure you have enough copies of the cartoons to give a complete set to each group of students.

IN CLASS   1 Divide the class into groups of three or four, and give each group a set of cartoons.

2 Tell the students to look carefully at the cartoons and to group them according to the subject matter of the humour; for example, the desert island situation, relations between men and women, politics, drunkenness, etc. The students' task is to work together and draw up a list of the different types of subject matter used.

3 Discuss one or two examples with the students, to make sure they understand the task.

4 The students work in groups, categorizing the cartoons and preparing their lists.

5 A spokesperson for each group reads the list to the class.

6 Write the different categories of subject matter mentioned by the students on the board. Then write the following questions on the board:
– *Are cartoons common in your country?*
– *If so, what is the most common subject matter?*
– *How are British/American cartoons similar to cartoons in your country?*
– *How are they different?*

7 Students work in groups, discussing the questions.

8 Follow-up with a whole-class discussion of the following questions:
– *What did you learn about British/American humour from this activity?*
– *What did you learn about humour in your own culture(s)?*

VARIATION

Intermediate level and above

Instead of focusing on the subject matter of the humour, students can draw up a list of visible aspects of British/American life contained in the cartoons, for example:
1 Houses and homes (rooms, furniture, etc.)
2 Work environments (offices, factories, etc.)
3 Leisure (fishing, reading, watching TV, etc.)
4 Eating and drinking (restaurants, pubs, etc.)
5 Travel (traffic, road signs, etc.)
6 Shopping (supermarkets, department stores, etc.)
7 Clothes and fashion (uniforms, hairstyles, etc.)

2.3 Culture composition

AIM

To improve composition skills; to stimulate recognition of cultural artefacts

MATERIALS

Realia and pictures

LEVEL

Intermediate and above

TIME

30–60 minutes

PREPARATION

From your travel abroad, from friends, or from magazines, collect realia such as bus or air tickets, bills, currency, exchange receipts, money, and photographs.

IN CLASS

1 Mix up the items so that they are in random order.

2 Divide the class into groups of two or three.

3 Tell the students you are going to hand round some items for them to identify.

4 Pass the items around. Each group identifies the ones they have. Students may ask another group if they are unsure.

5 Make sure that everybody knows what each item is.

6 Explain that each group is to make up a story about their set of items.

7 Each group then makes up a story and practises it for presentation to the rest of the class.

8 The groups tell their stories. Within a group, students can take turns to tell part of their story. As each item occurs in the story, it is shown to the class and then placed on a table.

9 When all the groups have finished, the students write their own individual versions of the story.

10 They can look at and share one another's versions if they wish.

REMARKS

If the students wish to work through Step 10, reassure them that there is no 'right' story. Details may vary, but what matters is that the writing should flow.

2.4. Currency deals

AIM

To familiarize the students with the currency of the target culture

MATERIALS

Coins and banknotes from the target country, tracing paper, glue, and card

LEVEL

Elementary

TIME

60 minutes

PREPARATION

1 Bring to class target-country coins and banknotes (or pictures of them). Also bring tracing paper, pencils, paste, and white card.

2 The students will need plain white paper.

IN CLASS

1 Explain the currency system and how it works, and show the money to the students.

2 Tell the class that they are going to 'forge' their own currency by copying the coins and notes you have brought.

3 Give out the coins, notes, and tracing paper. Each student either traces the design of the notes or makes a rubbing of the coin on the tracing paper.

4 They cut out and paste their designs on to card.

5 Call out the values of all the coins and banknotes at random, and ask the class to show you the appropriate coin or note.

6 The class can then 'buy' and 'sell' personal objects from each other, using the money they have made.

REMARKS   Keep the home-made currency for future use. It can be used to make a textbook activity more lively.

2.5 Front-page features

AIM   **To identify characteristic features of the front pages of British and/or American newspapers; to compare British and/or American front pages with the front pages of newspapers from the students' own countries; to practise note-taking**

MATERIALS   **Front pages of British and/or American newspapers and newspapers from the students' own countries**

LEVEL   **Lower-intermediate and above**

TIME   **60 minutes**

PREPARATION   1 Collect front pages of local, regional, or national newspapers from the UK and/or the US, and also front pages of newspapers from the students' own countries. Put the pages up around the walls of the classroom.

2 Make enough copies of the task sheet below to give one to each student.

IN CLASS   1 Explain to the class that by looking at the front page of a newspaper, they can learn a great deal about the values of the country that produced it. Tell the students that they are going to have a chance to compare the front pages of newspapers from different countries, to discover their similarities and differences.

2 Hand out the task sheets and explain that the students are to look carefully at the front pages displayed around the room, and make notes to try and answer the questions on the task sheet.

3 Allow enough time for the students to examine the front pages and make notes.

4 Then conduct a whole-class discussion based on the questions on the task sheet.

5 Conclude the activity with a feedback session. Ask the class:
- *What did you learn about British and/or American newspapers from this activity?*
- *What did you learn about newspapers from your own country?*

VARIATION

As an extension of this activity, students can be asked to compare the same front pages in terms of the number of advertisements and pictures, the amount of space given to local versus national/international news, etc.

TASK SHEET

---

1 How are the front pages from each country different from each other?

_____

_____

2 How are they similar?

_____

_____

3 What kinds of news do the editors in each country think is worth putting on the front page?

_____

_____

4 Look at the main news story and then at the other major news articles on each front page. Would the same news item be on the front page in your country? Why or why not?

_____

_____

2.6 Headlines

AIM

To familiarize the students with the conventions of newspaper headlines; to improve comprehension; to stimulate discussion

MATERIALS

Newspapers or magazines

LEVEL

Intermediate and above

TIME

20 minutes

PREPARATION

1 Collect enough headlines from newspapers and magazines for half the class.

2 Mount each headline on a piece of card for re-use. (For Variation 2, it is also worth mounting the stories themselves, without the headlines, on to separate pieces of card.)

3 Make a note of each headline and the story it introduces.

IN CLASS

1 Tell the students to work in pairs.

2 Give each pair a different headline, and ask them to work out what the headline means, and what the story behind it is.

3 The pairs then exchange stories with another pair.

4 Next, one student in each pair explains the headline to the rest of the class. The other tells the story behind the headline.

5 Confirm or correct as each pair finishes.

6 Finally, the class discuss what the choice of topic and wording of the headline tells them about the type of newspaper or magazine, the country of origin, and how it is different from headlines in the newspapers from their own culture.

VARIATION 1

1 If the students are already familiar with the British press, they can try to guess which newspaper each story comes from.

VARIATION 2

1 Give half the class a headline and the other half a story.

2 The students mingle and try to match up the headlines and the stories.

VARIATION 3

1 Give all the students the same story to study.

2 When they have all read it, ask them to write a headline for it.

3 Then show them the actual headline for the story. The students compare their headlines with the real one.

2.7 In my country

AIM

To encourage the transfer of cultural experience from L2 to L1; to improve discussion skills; to practise the conditional tense

MATERIALS

A video showing some cultural activity, for example, a baseball game in the US

LEVEL

Intermediate

TIME

30 minutes

PREPARATION

1 Select a video sequence of up to five minutes depicting a cultural event such as a ceremony, a sporting event, or a festival.

2 Prepare some comprehension questions to elicit information about the event.

3 Set up the VCR and monitor in the classroom.

IN CLASS

1 Write the following questions (or others which you have prepared) on the board:
– *Where is the event taking place?*
– *What is happening?*
– *Who are the people involved?*

2 Explain to the students that they are going to watch a video about a cultural event. After they have seen it, they are to answer the questions on the board.

3 The class watch the video.

4 Next, they answer the questions and discuss their answers in pairs.

5 Then explain that you want them to compare what they saw with a similar event in their country. Write on the board:
If this took place in your country:
– *What would happen?*
– *Who would be there?*
– *What would they wear?*
– *What time of year would it be?*
– *What would the weather be like?*

6 The students discuss how the situation would be different if the event were in their country. For example:
– *(If this were) In my country, we wouldn't play baseball, we would play football. The players would wear coloured shirts and shorts. They wouldn't use bats.* etc.

7 At the end of the class, ask the students to write about an event in their own country. Encourage them to use the conditional tense!

2.8 Meet the press

AIM
To raise awareness of the main newspapers and magazines in the target culture

MATERIALS
Newspapers and magazines

LEVEL
Elementary (Steps 1–5)
Intermediate and above (Step 6 and Variation)

TIME
30 minutes

PREPARATION
Collect enough mastheads (titles) of newspapers or magazines from the target culture to give one to each student.

IN CLASS
1 Distribute the mastheads among the students.

2 Ask them to say how much they think the newspaper costs, and whether it is a daily, weekly, or monthly publication.

3 Ask the students to say whether the masthead they have is large or small, and whether it has a logo or slogan on it.

4 Next, ask the class to decide which mastheads belong to 'quality' papers and which are from the 'popular' press.

5 Ask the class to decide what image the newspaper or magazine is trying to present.

6 Each student decides which newspaper or magazine in their own culture is the equivalent of the one they have been given.

VARIATION
If you are teaching within the target culture, your students might like to do a bit of research to find out the age, circulation, and reputation of each of the newspapers and magazines you have discussed.

REMARKS
Many books on Britain and America, and some coursebooks, contain illustrations of newspaper and magazine mastheads. Outside the target culture, newspapers and magazines may be obtainable from expatriates, embassies, and cultural missions. Newspapers and magazines such as the *Guardian Weekly*, the *European*, the *New York Herald Tribune*, *Time*, and *Newsweek* are now available in most countries.

2.9 Poems

AIM

To explore the cultural background of a poem

MATERIALS

Short poems

LEVEL

Intermediate and above

TIME

60 minutes

PREPARATION

1 Choose a short poem (10–20 lines), containing recognizable everyday language which sums up an attitude or feeling about life in the target culture. Poems by Roger McGough, Adrian Henri, Adrian Mitchell, and John Betjeman in Britain, and Ted Joans and Rod McKuen in the US are very suitable.

2 If possible, find a recording of the poem, or get a native speaker to record it for you.

3 Type out the poem in enough copies to give one to each student in the class.

4 If you are going to use a recording, set up the cassette player in the classroom.

IN CLASS

1 Read the poem aloud, or play the recording. Ask the students to write down an adjective that describes the mood of the poem.

2 Read or play the poem again. The class confirm or modify their opinions, and note down the parts of the poem which they feel justify their choice of adjective.

3 Give out the copies of the poem. Divide the class into groups, and ask each group to discuss one line.

4 Each group tells you the meaning of one line of the poem. Help them to resolve any discrepancies in interpretation.

5 The class then discuss the overall meaning of the poem and try to answer the question *What is the poet trying to say?*

6 Finally, ask the students to say in what way the poem reflects the target culture and the poet's attitude.

2.10 Radio news role-plays

AIM

To heighten awareness of the assumptions and perspectives of news reporters; to practise reading news articles; to practise speaking by presenting different versions of the same story through role-plays of news broadcasts; to practise listening to different versions of a news story

MATERIALS

A newspaper article on a national event in the target culture

LEVEL

Advanced

TIME

60 minutes

PREPARATION

Select a relatively short, easy newspaper article on a national event in the target culture. Make sure you have enough copies of the article to give one to each student.

IN CLASS

1 Divide the class into groups of two or three students. Distribute the copies of the news article.

2 Explain the task to the students. Half of the groups are to read the news article and then write a brief radio news report for their home culture, describing what has happened in the target culture. The other groups are to write a radio news report for the target culture.

3 The students work in their groups, reading the news article and writing their radio news reports.

4 One member of each group role-plays a radio news announcer and reads the group's news report.

5 Next, conduct a whole-class discussion on the different perspectives presented by each group in its news report. The discussion should centre on the following questions:
– *How did the news reports for the home culture differ from the news reports for the target culture?*
– *In what ways, if any, were the reports similar?*

VARIATION

The role-plays can be recorded on video or audio-cassette and then played back for the class.

REMARKS

To increase motivation, select the most controversial topic you can find, and then treat it with delicacy and respect!

Acknowledgement
This activity is adapted from Joyce Penfield, 'In the news' in *The Media: Catalysts for Communicative Language Learning* (Reading, Mass.: Addison-Wesley, 1987), pp. 41–2.

2.11 Show and tell

AIM

To heighten awareness of one's own culture; to practise speaking about something characteristic of one's own culture; to encourage respect for the other students in the class, and for the cultures they represent

MATERIALS

No special materials other than the objects that the students choose to bring to class

LEVEL

Lower-intermediate and above

TIME

60 minutes (over two classes)

PREPARATION

No special preparation is needed.

IN CLASS

Day 1

1 Tell the students that they are going to have an opportunity to show and talk to the class about an object that is personally meaningful to them. Everyone is to bring to class something they value, and which has cultural meaning to them. (If anyone has difficulty finding an object, they can bring a picture of it instead.)

2 It may help to give some examples of the kind of object you mean: an article of clothing, a picture of a national monument, a book by a favourite author, a musical instrument, etc.

Day 2

1 Tell the class that they will have two minutes to show their object to the class and to talk about in English, and that everyone will have a chance to discuss what they have seen and heard at the end of the presentations.

2 The students present their objects within the two-minute limit.

3 When all the students have finished, write the following questions on the board:
– *What one personal thing have you learned about each person in the class?*
– *What one thing did you learn about each person's culture?*
– *What more would you like to know about the culture of each member of the class?*
– *What have you learned about your own culture in doing this activity?*

4 Allow enough time for the students to think about and write their answers to the questions.

5 Finally, conduct a whole-class discussion based on the questions. If your class is very large, the discussion can be carried out in groups.

2.12 Stamp detectives

AIM

To increase awareness of and interest in the target culture; to practise deducing information about the target culture from postage stamps

MATERIALS

Postage stamps issued by the target country

LEVEL

Elementary and above

TIME

30–40 minutes

PREPARATION

Assemble a selection of postage stamps issued by the target country. Country-specific sets (either cancelled or in mint condition) can be bought in stamp shops and hobby shops. Get as many different designs as possible, and enough to pass round four or five to each student.

IN CLASS

1 Introduce the activity by saying something like this: *Today you will have a chance to be detectives. I'm going to give each of you some stamps from the United States. Pretend you know nothing at all about the country and that you have only these stamps to tell you about it. Try to find out as much as you can about the US: what it like, what the people are like, and how they live.*

2 Distribute the stamps, giving four or five to each student. Tell the students they have twenty minutes to look at their stamps and to list as many clues as they can find.

3 The students work individually, making lists of clues.

4 Finally, the students take turns to report what they have found out to the class.

VARIATION

As a follow-up, students can be reminded that postage stamps are a form of advertising and, like all advertising, show only the best aspects of a product (or country). Students can be asked to think about what postage stamps do *not* show, by asking questions such as:
- *Why are these particular aspects of national life shown and emphasized?*
- *Why not others?*
- *What does this country seem to believe is its most important industry, product, or scene?*

REMARKS

Students may want to use encyclopaedias during this activity. We suggest that you veto this (along with the use of stamp catalogues), because they are inappropriate tools for true stamp detectives. We would, however, permit the use of dictionaries. Magnifying glasses would also be useful for close examination of the stamps.

Acknowledgement
This activity is described in an article by J. W. Reese in the October, 1968 issue (pp. 113–14) of *Grade Teacher*.

2.13 Today's TV schedule

AIM

To increase awareness of the types of TV programme broadcast in the UK/US; to compare them with those in the students' own country; to practise deducing information from TV schedules

MATERIALS

A TV schedule from a British or American newspaper, and a task sheet for each student

LEVEL

Intermediate and above

TIME

60 minutes

PREPARATION

Photocopy the task sheet below, and make sure you have enough TV schedules from a UK/US newspaper to give one to each student.

IN CLASS

1 Distribute the task sheets and schedules. Then divide the class into groups of three or four.

2 Explain the task to the students. They are to work together in groups, studying the schedule and answering the questions on the task sheet.

3 Ask for one person in each group to report the group's answers.

4 Follow up with a whole-class discussion based on these questions:
– *What, if anything, surprised you?*
– *In what ways is the schedule different from a TV schedule in your country?*
– *In what ways is it similar?*
– *What did you learn about TV programming in the UK/US from this activity?*

VARIATION

Give the students copies of TV schedules from British and American papers. Ask them to look for the differences and similarities in content and organization of television in the two countries. As the students suggest them, draw up lists of similarities and differences on the board.

TASK SHEET

TODAY'S TV SCHEDULE

Use the information in the TV schedule to answer the following questions.

1 How many channels (separate broadcasting stations) can viewers choose from?

2 During what hours do these channels broadcast?

3 Do any of the channels seem to specialize in particular types of programmes? Which channels? What programmes?

4 Which programmes are documentaries?

5 Which are news programmes?

6 Which are sports programmes?

7 Which are for children?

8 Which are do-it-yourself programmes (for example, cooking, gardening, home repairs, etc.)?

9 Are any of the programmes in a language other than English? If so, which ones? In which languages?

Photocopiable © Oxford University Press

2.14 Topics in the news

AIM

To experience listening to the news from an American/British perspective; to practise identifying topic changes in a radio news broadcast

MATERIALS

Audio recording of a two- to four-minute sequence from a radio news broadcast

LEVEL

Lower-intermediate and above

TIME

30–45 minutes

PREPARATION

1 Make a brief (two- to four-minute) audio recording of an up-to-date radio news broadcast, covering several global topics.

2 Set up the cassette player in the classroom.

IN CLASS

1 Tell the students that you are going to play a recording of a radio news broadcast. Their task is to listen to the broadcast and summarize the different topics that are mentioned in the broadcast. Explain that you will play the recording three times. The first time, they are to identify each point at which a new topic is introduced. The second time, they are to write one or two words that summarize each topic. The third time, they are to write a complete sentence that summarizes what each topic is about.

2 Play the entire recording straight through. The students identify each point at which a new topic is introduced by raising their hands.

3 Replay the recording, stopping after each topic is mentioned. Ask for volunteers to offer one or two words that summarize the topic. Write the words on the board.

4 Play the recording a third time. Stop after each topic is mentioned, and allow enough time for students to write a complete sentence, summarizing what the topic is about.

5 Ask the students to work in pairs, comparing the sentences they have written.

6 Conduct a whole-class discussion about the topics and what they reveal about the target culture. The following questions can serve as focus points:
- *What topics were mentioned?*
- *What regions of the world were mentioned?*
- *What do the topics presented reveal about the target culture?*
- *In what ways would a radio news broadcast in your country be similar?*
- *In what ways would a radio news broadcast in your country be different?*

REMARKS

Recordings of global news items are recommended for this activity, since learners of English will probably find them easier to understand than local or national news items. With lower-intermediate students, adapted news broadcasts (for example, the BBC World Service or Voice of America broadcasts for learners of English) can be used.

VARIATION 1

Advanced students can be asked to write and produce their own news broadcasts for the class, based on national or international events.

VARIATION 2

A controversial topic mentioned on the news broadcast can serve as the focus of a debate on the issues involved. For example, in a news item about global warming, the students can argue for and against the following proposition: *Governments should wait for more evidence before taking energy-reduction measures to prevent global warming.*

VARIATION 3

Students can be asked to write a brief (one-page) paper, summarizing their personal reaction to an item mentioned in the broadcast.

VARIATION 4

As a follow-up, students can be asked to use magazines, books, and newspapers to find out more about one of the topics presented in the broadcast. They then write a brief (one-page) report, summarizing the information they gathered.

Acknowledgement
This activity is adapted from Joyce Penfield, 'Around the clock, around the world' in *The Media: Catalysts for Communicative Language Learning* (Reading, Mass.: Addison-Wesley, 1987), pp. 40–1.

3 Examining patterns of everyday life

Every culture offers distinct options, and exhibits distinct patterns associated with areas of everyday life such as employment, housing, and shopping. As increasing numbers of learners have the opportunity to travel, work, and study in English-speaking countries, they need to become aware of the lifestyles of people in these cultures: what people in these countries do in the common situations which are a part of normal everyday experience. The activities in this section are intended not only to reveal information about the lifestyles current in English-speaking cultures and the patterns usually followed by members of these cultures, but also to encourage comparison and discussion of how these options and patterns may be similar to or different from those in the students' culture. In this way, students arrive at a deeper understanding of both English-speaking cultures and their own, and they are better prepared to communicate with native speakers and handle the everyday situations they are likely to encounter in English-speaking countries.

Several of the activities in this section, such as 'Help wanted' (3.5), require the students to use authentic sources such as newspaper advertisements or video clips to gather information and deduce facts about everyday life in English-speaking countries. In other activities, for example 'Dating customs' (3.2), factual information about everyday customs and habits in English-speaking countries is presented in the form of a task sheet which the students use as a basis for cross-cultural comparison and discussion. In other activities, such as 'Is it true that . . .?' (3.8), students are given the opportunity to evaluate their own perceptions of everyday cultural patterns in English-speaking countries and to modify any misconceptions they may have.

All of the activities in this section can be used effectively in either monolingual or multilingual classes. 'Family trees' (3.4) and 'The house I grew up in' (3.11) are especially suitable for classes where the students come from a variety of cultural backgrounds. In classes where all the students come from the same culture, these two activities can also be very useful as a means of increasing awareness of the diversity which exists within the students' own culture, and of individual students' concepts of such culturally relevant themes as *family* and *home*.

3.1 Agony aunt

AIM

To compare personal/social problems in the UK/US and in the students' culture(s)

MATERIALS

'Agony aunt' letters from newspapers

LEVEL

Intermediate and above

TIME

50 minutes

PREPARATION

Cut out enough 'agony aunt' letters from newspapers to give one to each group of students.

IN CLASS

1 Explain that newspapers in the UK/US often contain columns in which an adviser—usually female—replies to published letters asking for advice about personal problems. It may be helpful to read an example of a published letter and a reply. For example:

Marjorie answers your problems

Q Dear Marjorie: My husband had too much to drink last night and confessed that the reason he bought me a pair of expensive pair of ear-rings for Valentine's Day was that he had bought some for his girlfriend and felt guilty. Now I don't even want the ear-rings. What do you think?   D. L.

A *Dear DL: I think that your husband should stop drinking and looking at ear-rings.*

2 Divide the class into groups of three or four. Give each group a letter.

3 Explain to the students that they are to read the letter and decide what advice they would give to the writer.

4 The students work in groups, reading the letters and making up their replies.

5 A volunteer from each group reads their letter and the group's reply.

6 Lead a whole-class discussion on the following questions:
– *What kinds of problems do people write about?*
– *Do newspapers in your country have similar advice columns?*
– *If so, what kinds of people are most likely to write letters to them?*
– *What problems are they most likely to write about?*

VARIATION

As an extension of this activity, read the letters, together with the original published replies. After reading each reply, ask the class the following questions:
– *Is the reply what you expected?*
– *Did anything in the reply surprise you?*
– *Would this reply be appropriate in your country? If not, why not?*

3.2 Dating customs

AIM

To compare relationships between men and women in the UK and the US with relationships between men and women in the students' culture(s)

MATERIALS

A task sheet for each student

LEVEL

Lower-intermediate and above

TIME

20–25 minutes

PREPARATION

Photocopy the task sheet overleaf. Make enough copies to give one to each student.

IN CLASS

1 Explain to the class that they are going to compare relationships between men and women in the UK and the US with relationships between men and women in their own culture(s).

2 Divide the class into pairs, and distribute the task sheet.

3 The students work in pairs, discussing the customs listed on the task sheet, and indicating whether each practice is the same or different in their culture. If the custom is different, they make brief notes explaining the difference.

4 Following the pairwork, volunteers take turns to report their answers to the class.

5 Follow up with a whole-class discussion on the following questions:
– *What have you learned about relationships between men and women in the UK and the US from this activity?*
– *Can you make any generalizations about relationships between men and women in the UK and the US?*
– *In what ways are the relationships different from the relationships in your culture?*
– *In what ways are they similar?*

VARIATION

As homework, you could ask the students to write a short composition, comparing and contrasting behaviour between men and women in the UK and US with behaviour between men and women in their culture.

TASK SHEET

DATING CUSTOMS

The statements below give information about the relationships between men and women in the UK and the US. Are these customs the same (**S**) or different (**D**) in your culture? Tick (√) the appropriate box. If a custom is different, write brief notes explaining the difference.

In the UK and the US   **In your culture**

	S	**D**
1 Young men and women go to parties together.	☐	☐

Notes

_____

_____

2 In their mid-teens (around the ages of fourteen or fifteen), boys and girls go on dates (to parties, dances, the cinema).	☐	☐

Notes

_____

_____

3 Parents very rarely choose dates for their children.	☐	☐

Notes

_____

_____

4 Teenagers usually date people of their own age, but sometimes girls date boys who are two or three years older.	☐	☐

Notes

_____

_____

5 A man often goes to collect his date at her home.	☐	☐

Notes

_____

_____

	S	D
6 Women may invite men to parties or other social events.	☐	☐

Notes

_____

_____

| 7 Teenagers meet members of the opposite sex at school, parties, or other social events. | ☐ | ☐ |

Notes

_____

_____

| 8 Men and women sometimes share expenses on a date. | ☐ | ☐ |

Notes

_____

_____

| 9 Teenagers and young adults meet and choose their own dates. | ☐ | ☐ |

Notes

_____

_____

| 10 Men and women sometimes date people of different economic, ethnic, social, or religious backgrounds. | ☐ | ☐ |

Notes

_____

_____

3.3 Early, on time, or late?

AIM	To compare the concepts of time in the UK and the US with the concept of time in the students' culture
MATERIALS	A task sheet for each student
LEVEL	Lower-intermediate and above
TIME	10–15 minutes
PREPARATION	Photocopy the task sheet opposite. Make enough copies to give one to each student.

IN CLASS

1 Explain to the class that the concept of time can be very different in different cultures, and that in this activity they are going to compare the concept of time in the UK and US with the concept of time in their own culture.

2 Divide the class into pairs, and distribute the task sheet.

3 The students work in pairs, discussing the events listed on the task sheet, and ticking their answers.

4 Following the pairwork, volunteers take turns to report their answers to the class.

5 Follow up with a whole-class discussion on the following questions:
- *What have you learned about the concept of time in the UK and the US from this activity? (In the UK and the US people are expected to arrive either early or on time.)*
- *What generalization can you make about the concept of time in the UK and the US? (Exact time-keeping is regarded as important in these countries.)*
- *In what ways, if any, is the concept of time in the UK and the US different from the concept of time in your culture?*

VARIATION

As a follow-up, you could ask the students to write five rules relating to time in the UK and the US, and five rules relating to time in their own culture. This can be done as pairwork in class or as homework.

REMARKS

The important point to bring out in the discussion phase (Stage 5) is that in the UK and the US people tend to arrange their lives and plan their activities around specific times. For example, while it is acceptable to arrive a few minutes early for a business meeting, it is considered extremely rude to arrive late.

ANSWER KEY

The events for which you should arrive early are 1, 2, 3, 5, 7, and 12.

The events for which you should arrive on time are 4, 6, 8, 9, 10, and 11.
You should not arrive late for *any* of the events listed!

TASK SHEET

Early, on time, or late?

Imagine that the following events take place in the UK or the US. Decide whether you should arrive early, on time (at exactly the time the event is scheduled), or late. Put a tick (√) in the appropriate column.

Event	Early	On time	Late
1 A business meeting			
2 A school examination			
3 A concert			
4 A date			
5 A job interview			
6 A meeting with a friend			
7 A film			
8 A graduation ceremony			
9 A dinner party			
10 A class			
11 A wedding			
12 A play			

3.4 Family trees

AIM	To increase awareness of how the concept of 'family' varies, depending on one's culture
MATERIALS	A drawing of a family tree
LEVEL	Lower-intermediate and above
TIME	30 minutes
PREPARATION	1 Prepare a drawing of a family tree on the board or on an overhead transparency. Include at least three generations in the drawing.

Photocopiable © Oxford University Press

2 If you are going to use transparencies, set up the overhead/slide projector and screen in the classroom.

IN CLASS

1 Use the model family tree to pre-teach or review the vocabulary for family relationships.

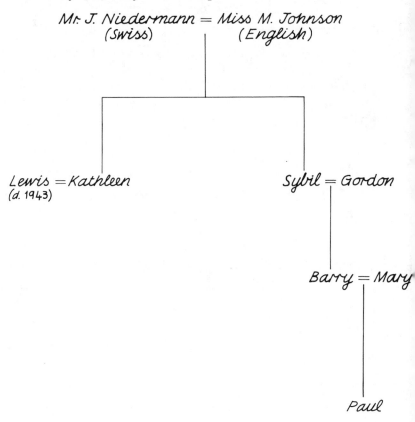

2 Ask the students to draw their own family trees on a piece of paper. Encourage them to be creative in their drawings, and to include all the people they consider to be part of their family.

3 The students work individually on their drawings.

4 Meanwhile, write the following questions on the board:
- *How many people are there in your family tree?*
- *How many generations are included in your family tree?*
- *Is the size of your family usual in your country?*
- *Where were your parents, grandparents, and great-grandparents born?*
- *In what ways are the family trees in your group similar?*
- *In what ways are they different?*

5 Next, divide the class into groups of three or four. The students compare their family trees, and use the questions on the board as the basis for the discussion.

6 Following the group discussion, ask the class the following questions, and allow them five minutes to think about their answers:
– *What did you learn about your idea of 'family'?*
– *Why are there differences in ideas about what makes up a family?*

7 Ask a student from each group to report the group's answers to the questions in Step 6.

VARIATION

Day 1

1 Show the students a photograph or slide of your own family. Ask the students to guess the family relationships among the different people in the picture.

2 Ask the students to bring a photograph of their family to the next class. (Students who do not have a photograph available can be asked to draw a picture of their family.)

Day 2

Follow Steps 4 to 7 above, substituting the word 'photograph' for 'tree'.

REMARKS

In classes where all the students are from one culture, this can still be an effective activity, as it increases awareness of diversity within their own culture and of individual students' concepts of 'family'.

3.5 Help wanted

AIM

To increase awareness of employment situations in the UK and the US; to practise deducing factual information from newspaper advertisements

MATERIALS

Examples of 'Help wanted' advertisements from British and/or American newspapers, and a task sheet for each student

LEVEL

Lower-intermediate and above

TIME

60 minutes

PREPARATION

Photocopy the task sheet below and collect 'Help wanted' advertisements from British and/or American newspapers. Make sure you have enough copies to give each student a task sheet and a complete set of the advertisements.

EXAMPLES

US

MARKETING MANAGER

We are looking for an experienced marketing professional to manage the promotion of our new range.

The ideal candidate will have at least three years' experience in marketing management, and will be a result-oriented leader with creative, organizational, and communications skills.

This is an outstanding opportunity and compensation will be dependent upon experience and results. We offer an attractive benefits package.

Please send resume to:
Personnel Department, Duluth Fashionwear,
200 Wydale Street, Lawrenceville, PA 67234

Graphics Associate

The in-house marketing department of an international company seeks a graduate part-time Graphics Associate with at least 2 years' typesetting experience with WordPerfect, IBM systems. Salary $28,000.
Send resume to Pat Clarke, 4097 Westport Road, Fairfield, CT60840.

TEACHER VACANCIES

Full & Part Time Positions
Certified applicants are sought for the following positions for the 1993–94 school year:
• Mathematics - Grades 9–12
• Special Education - Early Childhood
• Science - Grades 7–12
Closing date is May 30th.

Resumes with copies of certificates to: Dr. J. Delgado, Principal, Clapton Public Schools, 1387 West Street, Clapton, CT 20964

PHOTO STUDIO MANAGER

Outgoing, enthusiastic person wanted for photo studio in Falls Church. Spring and fall weekends, full time in summer. Sales and management experience a must. $7/hr + bonus. Artley Photographers. 202 776 4825

AU PAIR

Non-smoking female needed for live-in childcare. Northwest area. $100 wk. 462 4159

CHILDCARE (after school)

Friendship Heights, 2 girls, 6 and 8, 15-20 hours per week, M/F, own car, references required. Ideal for student, $8 per hour. Call 202 363 3158.

RESTAURANTS

The **Italian Straw Hat Restaurant** is now hiring M/F waiters, bartenders, cooks, dishwashers, and managers for its New England opening. Apply in person 9 a.m.-6 p.m. at 788 Flemming Road, Westport.

Bilingual Spanish operator required $7 per hour to start. Own transport 384 3094.

NANNY

Working couple seek fully trained nanny to live in and look after 2 year-old son. Require loving, dependable woman with excellent references and driving record. Must speak English. Hours 7.30 a.m. to 6.30 p.m. $150 /wk + free room, board, use of car. Please send application and resume to Ad 8375.

Market Researchers needed to conduct telephone studies. Evening and weekend shifts available. No exp nec. We train, good reading and pronunciation required. $145/wk. Call Maddison Inc 212 403 8827.

Secretary wanted for Pest Control company in Roxburgh. Hours approx 9 till 3 p.m. Could develop into 40-hour week. Must have basic secretarial skills, good phone manner, and be able to work independently. $7 /hr. Please call 974 3827 from 9 till 4 for appt.

DRIVERS

Seasonal help needed. Lots of work. $8/hr Must have reliable vehicle. Call 452 5552.

UK

A NEW CAREER IN SALES

You will be working for a well-established company selling gardening products to new and existing customers.

Own car essential.
Good career opportunities for the right candidate.
Starting salary £12,000 + car.
Interviewing immediately.

For details ring Mr. V. Hammond on 0323 503634.

SENIOR ARCHITECTURAL TECHNICIAN

with sound knowledge of building construction required for local firm of Architects. Experience of Computer-aided Design an advantage.
Telephone Rachel Patel on 0236 723493, or write with CV to:
Chambers Parslowe Bennett
65 High Street
Pemberton
Surrey

CREDIT CONTROL ASSISTANT

We have a vacancy for a Credit Control Assistant to provide back-up and clerical support to the Credit Controller.

Must be familiar with word-processing, able to work on own initiative, and have good telephone manner. Previous experience would be an advantage but full training will be given.

Salary £6,000–7,000, depending on experience. Additional benefits include flexitime, company pension scheme and subsidised staff restaurant.

Apply in writing with CV to Jean Forsythe, Personnel Manager, Cappa Ltd, Banbury OX23 4QT.

MANAGER

Benson's Carvery

A lively person with energy and enthusiasm is required for our busy city centre restaurant. Must have at least three years' experience in catering, and be good with people. A qualification in catering management would be an advantage.

Salary £16,000.
Closing date for applications Friday June 2nd.
Please ring 244044 for further information.

GENERAL VACANCIES

CARPENTER
Experienced part-time/full-time/freelance needed for structural conversion work. £8 per hour. 081 398 9460, 6-8 p.m.

ELECTRICIAN required due to expansion for servicing of Catering Equipment. Duties include providing estimates. Company van provided, salary negotiable. Contact Alan Bream on 0893 83219.

DOMESTIC

NANNY Mature, fun, house-proud nanny required to look after two children aged 6 and 3. Must be able to cook and swim. Salary to be negotiated. Own room/bath/car. Tel 0865 794389.

COMPANION good-humoured, gentle, caring woman 35–55 required by disabled lady for light household duties, cooking, reading, and friendship. £100 per week plus own room, use of car. Box 36.

IN CLASS

1 Distribute the task sheet and the advertisements, and divide the class into groups of three or four.

2 Explain the task to the students. They are to work together in their groups, reading the advertisements and using the information in them to complete the task sheet. Clarify students' questions about the vocabulary or the categories listed on the task sheet.

3 The students work in groups, reading the advertisements and completing the task sheet.

4 After the groups have completed the task sheet, ask for volunteers to report on their group's entries in each of the categories on the task sheet.

5 Follow up with a whole-class discussion on the following questions:
– *What did you learn about employment in the UK and/or the US from this activity?*
– *Are 'Help wanted' advertisements common in your country?*
– *If so, how are the advertisements in your country similar to those in British/American newspapers?*
– *How are they different?*

REMARKS

Almost any type of newspaper advertisement can be used to deduce facts about daily life and to get information about the values of the target culture. For other activities using advertisements, see 'Housing available' (3.7), 'Lost and found' (6.6), and 'What would you like to do?' (3.12).

TASK SHEET

HELP WANTED

Use information in the 'Help wanted' advertisements to find out as much as you can about the various types of employment available. Write the information you find under the appropriate heading.

Jobs which pay an hourly wage

_____

_____

_____

Jobs which pay a salary

_____

_____

_____

Jobs with prestige

_____

_____

_____

Facts about working hours

_____

_____

_____

Benefits or 'extras' (health insurance, holidays with pay, etc.)

_____

_____

_____

Labour organizations/trade unions

_____

_____

_____

Qualifications required

_____

_____

_____

Other information

_____

_____

_____

3.6 Holiday photographs

AIM
To encourage description; to highlight items for cultural comparison; to improve conversation skills

MATERIALS
Family or holiday photographs which show a variety of people and settings

LEVEL
Elementary and above

TIME
20 minutes

PREPARATION
Go through your holiday photograph album and choose pictures with a cultural feature which can be compared with a feature in the students' culture(s). For example, photographs from a holiday in the west of Ireland might feature local people, landscapes, farms, horses and carts, telephone boxes, signposts in Gaelic, ancient Celtic monuments, etc.

IN CLASS

1 Introduce the topic and the photographs. You might say: *This year I went on holiday to Ireland. Here are some of my holiday photographs.*

2 As a warm-up before the students see the pictures, ask them to call out some words that sum up their impressions of Ireland.

3 Ask the students to work in pairs or small groups.

4 Go round the groups and hand out one picture to each group. At the same time, give a brief commentary on each one. For example:
– *This is an Irish telephone box.*
– *This is the mountain scenery near Kerry.*

5 The groups then discuss the photographs, and look for cultural differences between what they see and life in their country.

6 Next, the students give you their impressions and feedback on any cultural feature they notice. For example, they might say: *Ireland is green. I thought it was grey. They use the word 'telefon'.*

7 At the end of the activity, summarize on the board the key differences and similarities found by the students, and list any new vocabulary.

REMARKS

Holiday photographs, whether yours or a friend's, are an immediate and useful way of giving learners an impression and sense of the culture they are learning about.

3.7 Housing available

AIM

To increase awareness about the variety, size, structure, and related features of housing in the UK and the US; to practise deducing factual information from newspaper advertisements

MATERIALS

Copies of property and real-estate advertisements from British and/or American newspapers, and a task sheet for each student

LEVEL

Lower-intermediate and above

TIME

60 minutes

PREPARATION

Photocopy the task sheet below. Collect property and real-estate advertisements from British and/or American newspapers. Make sure you have enough copies to give each student a task sheet and a complete set of advertisements.

EXAMPLES

STONESFIELD
£121,500

Stone semi-detached barn conversion, 2 receptions, 5 bedrooms. Quiet position not far from village centre.
0993 298571.

Hampstead

Light, pretty top floor 2-bed flat for sale or rent. Own entrance, 1 reception, gas CH, bath, kitchen.

**£110,000 or £600 pcm.
071 435 6661.**

Long Hanborough
£63,500

Victorian cottage, 2 beds 2 receptions. Night storage heaters, garage.
0993 698235

CHALGROVE

Bungalow, 2 bedrooms, 1 reception room, looking onto meadows and hills.

Offers over £68,000.
Phone 0865 241234 to view.

STANDLAKE Compact fully furnished 2 bed flat. One year let £300 pcm. Ring 880375 after 6 p.m.

OSNEY ISLAND Delightful Victorian terrace house, beautifully furnished, three beds, gas CH, garden. Available immediately for one year minimum. £600 pcm plus services. 0865 794183.

RURAL LOCATION Five bedroom country cottage in 3 acres of rolling woodland. To let furnished from August, £1250 pcm. Contact Grosvenors, Abingdon 66824.

ATLANTIC BEACH 3 BR HOME Vacation or year-round home on bay block close residents' private beach. Ocean views. All appliances. $21,000. Call (609) 984 9873.

FLORIDA PALM GREENS 2 BR/2 BTH Furnished 2nd fl appt. Pool, tennis, golf. $48K. Call (619) 759 9087 eve.

UPPER NEW YORK STATE Contemporary home on 3 acres near State park, spectacular views Hudson River. 5 BR 3 BTH, loft, deck, pool. $590,000. (914) 365 3800.

BEACON 3 BR/1.5 BTH Bilevel townhouse All appliances, patio. $850 mo + utilities. Available 15 April. (914) 962 3167.

PALM BEACH HOMES Homes, condominiums on the ocean, river, and golf courses from $175,000. (619) 553 8694.

GEORGETOWN, D.C. Family home, 5 BR/2 BTH, appliances, loft, deck, yard + basement 1 BR appt. $320,000. Call (202) 362 3158.

TACOMA PARK MD Attractive 2 BR/2 BTH townhouse. Available August for 1 year. $850 mo. Call (301) 565 0117 eve.

ROCK HILL N.Y. $245,000. Fabulous 5 BR 4 BTH residence on quiet tree-lined street. By appt only. Call (914) 385 2846.

ACORN FARM 2.5 acres Ranch style 3 BR/2 BTH screen porch, brick frplc, open deck, double garage. $129,000. (717) 775 7539.

FAIRFIELD Exceptional 3 BR 2.5 BTH colonial hse, den beaut landsc. Available Jul/Aug $1,000 mo. Call (203) 255 5525.

UK   **US**

IN CLASS

1 Distribute the task sheet and the advertisements, and divide the class into groups of three or four students.

2 Explain the task to the students. They are to work together in their groups, reading the advertisements and using the information in them to complete the task sheet.

3 Allow enough time for the groups to read the advertisements and complete the task sheet.

4 After the groups have finished, ask for volunteers to report on the information which their groups found for each heading on the task sheet.

5 Follow up with a whole-class discussion on the following questions:
– *What did you learn about housing in the UK and/or the US from this activity?*
– *What other things did you learn about daily life in the UK and/or the US?*
– *What did you learn that is different from the situation in your culture?*

REMARKS

Almost any type of newspaper advertisement can be used to deduce facts about daily life and to get information about the values of the target culture. For other activities using advertisements, see 'Help wanted' (3.5), 'Lost and found' (6.6), and 'What would you like to do?'(3.12).

TASK SHEET

HOUSING AVAILABLE

Use the information in the advertisements to list as many facts as you can about the types of housing described in the advertisements. Write down the information under the appropriate heading.

Types of housing available (studios, terraced houses, bungalows, etc.)

_____

_____

_____

Sizes of houses and flats (number of rooms, total area, etc.)

_____

_____

_____

Price (of rent, purchase, etc.)

_____

_____

_____

Types of heating

_____

_____

_____

Other information

_____

_____

_____

3.8 Is it true that...?

AIM

To develop the ability to evaluate and refine generalizations about the target culture

MATERIALS

A photocopied list of generalizations about the target culture

LEVEL

Upper-intermediate and above

TIME

40–50 minutes

PREPARATION

Compile a list of eight to ten generalizations about the target culture. Some should be true and some should be false (see the sample list below). Make enough copies of the list to give one to each student.

SAMPLE HAND-OUT

SOME GENERALIZATIONS ABOUT US CULTURE

1 Most young people in the US start dating around the age of twelve.

2 The bill in most restaurants in the US includes a service charge.

3 In the US, shopping for groceries is usually done by going to a supermarket once a week.

4 Most Americans do their own housework.

5 In American cities, people who walk their dogs in public are required to clean up after them.

6 It is polite to ask Americans questions about their salary.

7 When invited to a birthday party in the US, you are expected to give a gift of money.

8 In the US, saying 'Thank you' is a common way of reacting to a compliment.

9 The cost of university tuition is so expensive in the US that only the very rich can afford it.

IN CLASS

1 Divide the class into pairs and distribute the hand-out to the students.
2 Make sure that the students understand the statements.
3 Tell the students that they are to mark each statement either:
   a. (probably true)
   b. (probably false)
   c. (I don't know).
Where the students mark the statements (a) or (b), they are to make brief notes on the evidence that supports their answer. Where they mark them (c), they are to indicate what specific information they need in order to make a judgement.

4 Students work in pairs, discussing the statements, marking them, and making notes.

5 Following the pair work, volunteers report their answers and supporting comments to the class. Indicate whether you feel that the comments are strong enough to support the judgements. If necessary, correct any misconceptions based on limited evidence.

VARIATION

As homework, students can be asked to prepare a brief written report, summarizing the evidence (from library sources and/or target-culture informants) which confirms, contradicts, or modifies one or several of the statements.

REMARKS

This is a good testing format. Students should be graded on the strength of their supporting arguments, *not* on the basis of whether they answered (a), (b), or (c).

ANSWER KEY

Answer key to sample hand-out
The generalizations that are most true about US culture are 3, 4, 5, and 8. Items 1, 2, 6, 7, and 9 are false.

Acknowledgement
This activity is a variation on a technique described in H. N. Seelye, *Teaching Culture* (Lincolnwood, Il.: National Textbook Company, 1988).

3.9 Shopping habits

AIM

To compare shopping habits in the UK and the US with shopping habits in the students' culture(s)

MATERIALS

A task sheet for each student

LEVEL

Lower-intermediate and above

TIME

20–25 minutes

PREPARATION

Photocopy the task sheet below. Make enough copies to give one to each student.

IN CLASS

1 Explain to the class that they are going to compare shopping habits in the UK and US with shopping habits in their own culture(s).

2 Divide the class into pairs and distribute the task sheet.

3 The students work in pairs, discussing the statements on the task sheet, and noting whether the practice is the same or

different in their culture(s). If it is different, they should write brief notes explaining the difference.

4 Following the pairwork, volunteers take turns to report their answers to the class.

5 Follow up with a whole-class discussion on the following questions:
- *What have you learned about shopping habits in the UK and the US from this activity?*
- *In what ways are shopping habits in the UK and the US different from shopping habits in your culture?*

ASK SHEET

SHOPPING HABITS

The statements below give information about shopping habits in the UK and the US. Are these habits the same (**S**) or different (**D**) from the shopping habits of the people in your culture? Put a tick (√) in the appropriate boxes. If any of the habits are different, write brief notes explaining the differences.

In the UK and the US   **In your culture**

                                   S   **D**

1 Adults do most of their own   ☐   ☐
  shopping for clothes.
                                  Notes

                                  _____

                                  _____

2 Mothers usually buy all the   ☐   ☐
  clothes for the young
  children in the family.   Notes

                                  _____

                                  _____

3 Teenagers usually choose   ☐   ☐
  their own clothes.
                                  Notes

                                  _____

                                  _____

4 Married couples usually   ☐   ☐
  shop for large items such as
  cars, furniture, and TV sets   Notes
  together.
                                  _____

                                  _____

	S	D
5 Shopping for groceries is usually done by going to the supermarket once a week.	☐	☐

Notes

_____

_____

6 Shops do not close for lunch, and some stay open till 7.00 p.m. or later on certain days, especially in big cities.	☐	☐

Notes

_____

_____

7 Department stores and grocery stores are open all day on Saturdays.	☐	☐

Notes

_____

_____

8 In families, it is often the mother who does most of the food shopping.	☐	☐

Notes

_____

_____

9 Many oven-ready (frozen or micro-wavable) items are available in supermarkets.	☐	☐

Notes

_____

_____

10 Many people buy bread, cakes, biscuits, and pies in a supermarket rather than in a bakery.	☐	☐

Notes

_____

_____

3.10 Same or different?

AIM

To compare and contrast features of the target culture with features of the students' culture(s)

MATERIALS

A short video sequence

LEVEL

Elementary and above

TIME

20–25 minutes

PREPARATION

Select a short (one- to three-minute) video sequence which illustrates several features of the target culture which are likely to be different in the students' own culture(s).

IN CLASS

1 Ask the students to take a sheet of paper and draw a line down the middle. At the top of the sheet on one side of the line, they write the word *same*. On the other side of line, they write the word *different*.

2 Tell the students that you are going to play a video sequence which contains information about the target culture. Their task is to find three things that are the same in their country as what they see in the video sequence, and three things that are different.

3 Play the sequence twice. The first time, the students watch. The second time, they make notes.

4 After they have watched the sequence, divide the students into small groups to discuss the similarities and differences they have observed. In monocultural classes, students can compare their lists and come up with a definitive one.

5 Ask individual students to report to the class, listing all the similarities and differences they observed between what is shown on the video and their own culture.

REMARKS

This technique can be used with almost any video sequence which clearly illustrates features of the target culture. Sequences involving cultural rituals (for example, weddings, birthdays, courtroom scenes, cocktail parties, etc.) work especially well.

VARIATION

1 As an extension to this activity, students can be asked to watch target-language TV programmes (via satellite broadcast if outside the target-language culture) on their own. This would be an on-going project. The students would look for and report on similarities to their own cultures.

2 Tell the students to start by looking for a difference—since it will probably be easier to notice—and then look for a similarity that underlies the difference. For example, one Chinese student

reported the following perceptions of the TV programme 'Perry Mason':

Different

When people in the US talk to each other, they look at the other person's eyes. In China, we wouldn't look straight at the other person's eyes.

When people meet, they hug and kiss. In China, people would shake hands or nod their heads.

Same

The Americans and the Chinese both think it is polite to listen carefully to the other person.

Both the Americans and the Chinese do something physical to show they are happy to meet another person.

Acknowledgement
We learned this variation from Paul Arcario.

3.11 The house I grew up in

AIM	**To increase awareness of the fact that culture plays a role in how people define and create their homes; to see how different cultures organize and use their homes**
MATERIALS	**No special materials are needed**
LEVEL	**Elementary and above**
TIME	**60 minutes**
PREPARATION	No special preparation is needed.
IN CLASS	1 Draw a floor plan of your home on the board. Include the names of the rooms and important furniture, and show where the doors are. Use the floor plan to pre-teach or recycle the vocabulary for housing and furniture.

2 Explain the task to the class. The students are to draw a floor plan of their house (or the house they grew up in). Tell the students to include the names of the rooms and important furniture, and indicate where the doors are.

3 The students work individually, drawing the floor plans.

4 Meanwhile, write the following questions on the board:
- *How many people live in this house?*
- *Which doors are usually open?*
- *Which are usually closed?*
- *Which are locked? When? Why?*

– Where are visitors entertained?
– Where do visitors sleep?
– Are there any spaces that belong to one member of the family?
  Which spaces? Which family member?
– Does the house have a front garden? A back garden? A fence?

5 Divide the class into groups of three or four. Tell the groups
to compare their drawings and then to use the questions on the
board as a basis for discussion.

6 As a follow-up, conduct a whole-class discussion on the
following question:
– Why are there differences in different people's idea of home?

3.12 What would you like to do?

AIM	**To increase awareness of leisure-activity options in the UK and/or the US; to practise deducing information from newspaper advertisements; to discuss and compare one's personal preferences and interests**
MATERIALS	**Arts and entertainment advertisements from British and/or American newspapers/magazines, and a task sheet for each student**
LEVEL	**Intermediate and above**
TIME	**60 minutes**
PREPARATION	Photocopy the task sheet overleaf and make up a collection of advertisements for cinemas, theatres, concerts, museums, galleries, exhibitions, etc. from a British and/or American newspaper or magazine. Make sure you have enough copies to give each student a task sheet and a complete set of advertisements.
IN CLASS	**1** Tell the students that you are going to give them some arts and entertainment advertisements from a British and/or American newspaper/magazine. Their task is to imagine that they are in the city where the advertisements were published, and to choose the five events they would most like to attend.

2 Distribute the task sheet and the advertisements. The students
work individually on the task sheet.

3 Divide the class into groups of three or four. The groups
compare their task sheets and discuss the events they have
chosen, and their reasons for choosing them.

4 Follow up with a whole-class discussion of the following
questions:
– *Did any of the advertisements surprise you? Which ones? Why?*
– *Which advertisements might appear in newspapers in your own
   country?*
– *Which advertisements would not? Why not?*
– *What did you learn about the leisure activities of people in the UK
   and/or the US from this activity?*

TASK SHEET _____

WHAT WOULD YOU LIKE TO DO?

Look at the arts and entertainment advertisements. Imagine
that you are in the city where they were published. Choose the
five events you would most like to attend. List each event, and
your reason for choosing it below.

Events   **Reasons**

1 _____   _____

  _____   _____

  _____   _____

2 _____   _____

  _____   _____

  _____   _____

3 _____   _____

  _____   _____

  _____   _____

4 _____   _____

  _____   _____

  _____   _____

5 _____   _____

  _____   _____

  _____   _____

XAMPLES

GAUMONT CINEMA
WEST END

Access/Visa/Bookings 071 532 1001
All programmes bookable in advance.
Licensed bar.

DEADLY WEAPON

Programmes: 1:30, 3:45, 6:00, 8:45.
Late night shows Fri/Sat 11:30.

The Everlasting Story

Programmes: 2:30, 4:00

The Undead

Programmes: 6:30. 9:00.
Late night shows Fri/Sat 11:30.

Oxford Odeon

Friday May 30th
The Green Rabbits Plus The Hamstrings

Doors open 7pm Band on stage 8pm

Tickets £4 and £2
(students and unemployed)

Robin Malony
and his band

Thursday 29th May

THE BAT AND BALL,
High Street, Frampton

The best Folk venue in town!

SAN FRANCISCO OPERA

CARMEN (*Bizet*)
Season Premiere May 21, 22, 23
Conducted by Juan Fundera
With Katherine Mallett/Sally Miller/James Pereira

DIE ZAUBERFLÖTE (*Mozart*)
May 24, 25, 27, 28, 29, 31
Conducted by Christopher Jones
With Keith Stringer/Judith Mainwaring/Donald Spruce
With the Los Angeles City Orchestra

Call (415) 779-6655 or
Come to the Box Office

Cast subject to change. Evenings at 7:30, matinees at 2 except as noted. No refunds or exchanges.

Box Office hours: Sunday noon to 5:30, Monday through Saturday 10 to 7.

'TREMENDOUS... WONDERFUL CASTING'
DAILY MIRROR

'A STUPENDOUS PRODUCTION'
IRISH TIMES

JUNO AND THE PAYCOCK

BY **SEAN O'CASEY**

WITH
MARK HUGHES

'SHOULD ON NO ACCOUNT BE MISSED'
NEW YORK TIMES

Only 45 performances - 24 May - 16 July
EVERYMAN THEATRE, HAMPSTEAD
BOX OFFICE 081 776 2845
CREDIT CARDS 081 776 3829

Arts Council Funded

---

4 Examining cultural behaviour

The unifying concept underlying all the activities in this section is the goal of increasing awareness of and sensitivity to culturally different modes of behaviour. In the contemporary teaching of English as a second or foreign language, more and more attention is being paid to culturally appropriate behaviour—what native speakers of English say and do in specific social situations. However, if learners of English are to communicate successfully on a personal level with individuals from English-speaking cultures, they need not only to recognize the different cultural patterns at work in the behaviour of people from English-speaking countries; they also need to become aware of the ways in which their own cultural background influences their own behaviour, and to develop a tolerance for behaviour patterns that are different from their own. For this reason, the activities in this section include not only information-oriented activities which present facts about culturally appropriate behaviour in English-speaking countries, but also activities oriented towards experiential learning and the growth of self-awareness.

All of the activities in this section encourage students to become more aware of the subtleties of cultural behaviour. In 'Video observation' (4.10), and 'What did he do? What did she say?' (4.11), video is used as a means of expanding students' ability to identify observable cultural features of the target culture. 'Mini-surveys' (4.6) involves students interviewing native speakers as a source of information about typical behaviour in English-speaking cultures. Some activities, 'Culture assimilators' (4.4), for example, ask students to examine culturally sensitive situations and choose the most appropriate behaviour for that situation. Still other activities—'Critical incidents' (4.2) and 'Cross-cultural role-plays' (4.3)—highlight misunderstandings experienced by people in cross-cultural situations, and ask students to identify the cultural factors at work and then to propose their own solutions to the problems involved. 'Observation and judgement' (4.8) focuses on getting students to realize how their own observations may be affected by their past experience and cultural background.

With the exception of 'Answering real questions' (4.1), which is designed for use in a class composed of students from different cultures, all of the activities in this section can be carried out in both monolingual and multilingual classes. In some cases, as with

'Culture assimilators' (4.4), once students become familiar with the specific technique, they can be encouraged to go beyond the situations illustrated and to draw on their own experiences and discuss topics of particular interest concerning differences in cultural behaviour.

4.1 Answering real questions

AIM

To increase knowledge and awareness of the individual cultures represented by the class; to practise writing questions about a specific culture; to practise speaking about one's culture to a group

MATERIALS

Large sheets of paper and crayons (or felt-tip pens)

LEVEL

Elementary and above

TIME

Variable (part of several class periods, plus extra-curricular time)

PREPARATION

1 Bring to class a large sheet of paper for each country represented in the class. At the top of each sheet of paper write the name of each of the countries. Be sure to include a sheet for the target culture, and/or your own country, so that the students will have the opportunity to question you.

2 Pin up the sheets around the walls of the classroom.

3 Assemble enough crayons or felt-tip pens to give one to each student in the class.

4 If you think the students intend to use slides, set up the slide projector and screen in the classroom on the day of the students' presentations.

IN CLASS

1 Explain the task to the students. They are to move from paper to paper and write the questions they wish to ask about each country. For example, all questions about Egypt should be written on the paper marked 'Egypt'. Students may write as many questions as they like.

2 After the students have finished writing their questions, divide the class in to groups, according to the countries represented by the individual students. For example, all the students from Egypt will make up one group. Explain that the members of each group are to work together and prepare their answers to the questions written about their country.

3 Distribute the papers with the questions and assign the groups part of a class period to answer the questions written about their country. Tell the groups to meet outside class to plan their

presentations. Explain that they are not to write out a speech and read it. They may use notes, but they are to speak spontaneously. Encourage groups to use visual aids (slides or photographs) in their presentations.

4 Allow a few minutes for the groups to read over the questions and to ask for clarification on anything that has been written.

5 Over several class periods, groups take turns to make their presentations. The length of individual presentations will vary, depending on the linguistic ability of the students and the number of questions each group has to answer. Try to plan one or two fifteen- to thirty-minute presentations per class.

6 After all the presentations have been made, conduct a whole-class discussion on the following questions:
- *What did you learn about the countries represented by the people in this class?*
- *What did you learn about your own country?*
- *In what ways, if any, did this activity change your opinion about any of the countries?*

4.2 Critical incidents

AIM

To increase awareness and sensitivity to cultural differences; to stimulate discussion and provide opportunities for students to express their views; to practise listening and/or reading skills

MATERIALS

A task sheet for each student

LEVEL

Intermediate and above

TIME

30 minutes

PREPARATION

Choose one of the task sheets below, and make enough copies to give one to each student. Alternatively, you may wish to develop your own cultural incidents, based on your experience.

IN CLASS

1 Introduce the subject of 'critical incidents' to the class by saying something like: *A critical incident is a situation where there is a communication problem between people of different cultures. In other words, something goes wrong because the people involved don't understand each other's culture.* Tell the students that they are going to read a critical incident and come up with their own solutions to the problem involved.

2 Distribute the task sheet and tell the students they are to work individually, reading about the incident and choosing their answers to each question.

TASK SHEET 1

ACCEPTING A COMPLIMENT

Read the situation below, and choose the best answers to the questions. Sometimes more than one answer is possible.

Linda, an American teacher in an adult class in the US, was speaking to Usa, one of her Thai students. She said, 'Usa, I'm very happy with your work. Your English is really improving.'

Usa looked down and said, 'Oh, no. I'm not a good student. My English is not very good.'

Linda really thought that Usa was making progress, and she wanted her to know it. She said to Usa, 'But you *are* a good student, and you're making excellent progress. You should be proud of your work.'

Usa responded to this remark saying, 'No, no. You are a very good teacher, but I am not a good student.'

Linda didn't know what to say, so she decided not to give Usa any more compliments.

1 Why did Usa look down when the teacher complimented her?

  a. She was ashamed of her work.
  b. She was embarrassed by the teacher's compliment.
  c. She was trying to show respect for the teacher.
  d. She didn't like the teacher.

2 Why did Linda decide not to give Usa any more compliments?

  a. She decided that Usa really was not a good student.
  b. Usa's behaviour was disrespectful.
  c. Usa didn't seem to be pleased with the compliment.
  d. She expected Usa to say something like 'Thank you'.

---

3 Allow enough time for the students to read about the incident and choose answers.

4 Next, divide the class into groups of three or four. The groups work together, discussing the incident and comparing their answers.

5 Meanwhile, write the following questions on the board:
– *What cultural values were involved?*
– *Who was at fault?*
– *What would you do in this situation?*

6 The groups continue to work together, discussing their answers to the questions on the board.

7 Lead a whole-class discussion of the incident and the various answers (see Answer Key on page 87). Focus on the cultural values involved, and whether or not the suggested solutions took these values into consideration. Discuss the potential outcomes of each suggested solution.

TASK SHEET 2

ADDRESSING THE TEACHER

Read the situation below, and choose the best answers to the questions. Sometimes more than one answer is possible.

It was the first day of the English class and the teacher was introducing himself. He wrote his full name, Alan Jones, on the board and said, 'My name is Alan Jones. If you like, you can use "Mr" with my name. Now I'd like you to tell me your names. Let's start with you,' he said, indicating a young woman in the front row.

The young woman answered, 'My name is Liliana Castro, but you can call me Lily, Teacher.'

Then the teacher said, 'OK. I'll call you Lily, but please don't call me "Teacher". Please call me Alan or Mr Jones.'

Lily looked confused, but the teacher ignored her and continued to ask the students to introduce themselves.

1 Why did Liliana call Alan Jones 'Teacher'?

   a. She didn't know his name.
   b. She was trying to show respect.
   c. She couldn't pronounce his name.
   d. She felt confused.

2 Why did Alan Jones ask Liliana not to call him 'Teacher'?

   a. He didn't really like being a teacher.
   b. He wanted to be friendly.
   c. In his country, only very young pupils call their teacher 'Teacher'.
   d. He thought Liliana was being rude.

ANSWER KEY

Task Sheet 1: Accepting a compliment

1 The most likely explanations are (b) and (c).
Usa may have felt uncomfortable at being singled out for such a compliment, and looking down is a mark of respect in many cultures.
2 The most likely explanations are (c) and (d).
It is normal for teachers in English-speaking countries to compliment students for good work, and for students to take the compliment with a 'Thank you'.

Task Sheet 2: Addressing the teacher

1 The most likely explanation is (b).
In many cultures students, no matter what their age, address their teachers as 'Teacher', in order to show respect.
2 The most likely explanation is (c).

ASK SHEET 3

ATTENDING A PARTY

Read the situation below, and choose the best answers to the questions. Sometimes more than one answer is possible.

Martha, an American teacher in the US, had just started teaching English to a group of Japanese students. She wanted to get to know the students more informally, so she invited them to her house for a party. The students all arrived together at exactly 8.00 p.m. They seemed to enjoy the party: they danced, sang, and ate most of the food. At about 10.00 p.m., one of the students said to the teacher, 'I think it's time for me to leave. Thank you very much for the party.' Then all the other students got up to go, and all left at the same time. Martha decided she would never invite *them* again!

1 Why did all the students leave together?

   a. They didn't like late nights.
   b. There was no more food.
   c. They were doing what was normal for them.
   d. They had an invitation to another party.

2 Why did Martha decide never to invite these students to her house again?

   a. She felt insulted, because they all left at once.
   b. They had eaten all the food.
   c. They stayed too late.
   d. They hadn't brought her a present.

ANSWER KEY

Task Sheet 3: Attending a party

1 The most likely explanation is (c).
Young people in Japan and many other countries in Asia often arrive at social events in a group and leave in a group.

VARIATION

Instead of a written description of a short critical incident, play a short video sequence in which there is a communication problem between a native English speaker and a person or persons from another culture. Films like *Gung Ho* and *Passage to India* contain many such incidents.

REMARKS

In the class-discussion phase (Step 8), it is not necessary to reach group consensus, but you may wish to point out that in a given situation one action may be more appropriate than another. As students become more familiar with the 'critical incident' technique, they can be encouraged to write up their own critical incidents for class discussion.

2 The correct answer is (a).
In the US and other English-speaking countries, 10.00 p.m. is
relatively early to leave a party.

4.3 Cross-cultural role plays

AIM	**To increase awareness of the types of misunderstanding that can occur between people of different cultures**
MATERIALS	**No special materials are needed** (simple props are optional)
LEVEL	**Intermediate and above**
TIME	**45 minutes**
PREPARATION	Prepare a brief description of an incident that happened to you and that led to a cross-cultural misunderstanding.
IN CLASS	1 Explain to the students that, at one time or another, most of us have been involved in situations that have led to cross-cultural misunderstandings. To make sure that the students understand what you mean, and to encourage recall of similar incidents in the students' own experience, describe a cross-cultural incident in which you were involved. For example, one of the authors of this book was staying overnight for the first time with a Japanese family. After dinner, she and her hosts sat in the living room and discussed a variety of things: the family's trips abroad, things the guest should be sure to see while in Japan, etc. As the night wore on, the hosts politely and repeatedly asked if she wanted to take her bath. The guest replied that she was in no hurry and could wait until later. What she failed to realize at the time was that her hosts were hinting that it was bedtime, and that she—as the guest—should take her bath first, so that the family members could then take theirs and retire.

2 Divide the class into groups of three or four. Students take
turns to describe cross-cultural incidents in which they were
involved.

3 Each group selects one of the incidents described. Together
they plan how to dramatize the incident. It is important that the
student involved in the original incident should not play his or
her own part.

4 Groups take turns to perform their role plays in front of the
class. The other students try to guess which student was actually
involved in the incident.

5 The whole class discusses each incident and its cross-cultural implications.

VARIATION

Instead of describing cross-cultural incidents to their groups, individual students can write up incidents that happened to them, and place their descriptions in a box. Small groups of students can draw an incident from the box and act it out. This can then be followed by a whole-class discussion.

4.4 Culture assimilators

AIM

To increase awareness of appropriate behaviour in English-speaking cultures; to compare and contrast these behaviour patterns with those in the students' own culture(s)

MATERIALS

A task sheet for each student

LEVEL

Intermediate and above

TIME

20–30 minutes

PREPARATION

Choose one of the task sheets overleaf. Make enough copies to give one to each student.

IN CLASS

1 Divide the class into groups of three or four.

2 Distribute the task sheet and explain the task to the students. They are to work together in groups, discussing the situations and deciding what they would do in each situation.

3 The groups work together, discussing the situations, and answering the questions.

4 After the students have completed the task sheet, a volunteer from each group summarizes the group's discussion and answers.

5 Tell the students to imagine that they are in the same situations in their home country. What would they do in each situation?

6 The students continue to work in groups, discussing the situations and saying what they would do in their home country.

7 After the students have had a chance to discuss their answers in small groups, conduct a whole-class discussion on the following questions:
 – *What did you learn about behaviour in English-speaking countries from this activity?*
 – *What did you learn about behaviour in your home country?*

VARIATION 1

As an extension of this activity, ask the students to tell the class about situations in which they did not understand someone's behaviour, or in which they were not sure how to behave. The groups can then suggest possible interpretations and solutions.

VARIATION 2

An answer key to the task sheets is provided below. Instead of asking the groups to report their discussion to the class (Step 4 above), you may wish to distribute the answer key and have the students continue their discussion in small groups, comparing their own answers with those in the answer key.

REMARKS

1 The situations on the task sheets are a sample of some of the intercultural problems common to recently-arrived foreign students in the UK and the US. They are intended to stimulate discussion and to lead students to explore questions of cultural differences that interest them.

2 As an alternative, you may wish to develop your own culture assimilators.

Acknowledgement
This activity is a variation of the culture-assimilator technique described in US Naval Amphibious School, 'Profile of cross-cultural readiness' in D. S. Hoopes and P. Ventura (eds.), *Intercultural Sourcebook* (LaGrange Park, Il.: Intercultural Network, Inc., 1979), pp. 89–101.

TASK SHEET 1

SOCIAL BEHAVIOUR

Work with a partner. Imagine that the situations below take place in an English-speaking country. What would you do in each situation? In some cases, more than one answer is possible.

1 You've been having digestive problems for a week, and have just started to feel better. You meet a British friend at a party. Your friend says, 'How are you?' What would you do?

   a. Start talking in detail about your problem.
   b. Say, 'Fine, thanks. How are you?'
   c. Say, 'Not bad, thanks. How are you?'
   d. Nothing.

2 You're visiting an American friend in her new apartment. You like the apartment and you want your friend to know. What would you do?

   a. Say, 'Your apartment is nice. How much is the rent?'
   b. Say, 'Gee, this place is really nice.'
   c. Say, 'I really like your apartment.'
   d. Say nothing, but show that you are interested by walking around, looking at everything in the apartment, and picking up everything that is movable.

---

3 You've been invited to dinner at a friend's home. You're about to sit down to eat, but you want to use the toilet first. What would you do?

   a. Say, 'Excuse me. Where's the toilet?'
   b. Say, 'Could I wash my hands before dinner?'
   c. Say, 'Do you mind if I use the bathroom?'
   d. Say nothing and start looking around the house for the toilet.

4 You're a guest in a British or American friend's home. Your friend asks if you would like something to drink. You really would like a drink. What would you do?

   a. Say, 'Yes, please.'
   b. Say, 'Yes, that would be lovely.'
   c. Say, 'No, thank you' and wait for your friend to ask you again.
   d. Say, 'That's OK. I can get it myself.'

5 You've just been introduced to a British or American friend's parents. What would you do?

   a. Say, 'Hello', and bow.
   b. Say nothing and shake hands.
   c. Say, 'Nice to meet you', and shake hands.
   d. Say, 'Hi!'

TASK SHEET 2

CLASSROOM BEHAVIOUR

Work with a partner. Imagine that the situations below take place in the UK or the US. What would you do in each situation? In some situations, more than one answer may be possible.

1 You're 20 minutes late for class. The teacher is explaining something to the class when you arrive. What would you do?

   a. Go in, walk up to the teacher and apologize.
   b. Wait outside the classroom until the class is over and then apologize to the teacher.
   c. Knock on the door and wait for the teacher to tell you it's OK to come in.
   d. Go in as quietly as you can and take a seat.

2 The teacher gives the class some homework for the next day. You know that you won't be able to finish it on time. What would you do?

   a. Explain the situation to the teacher and ask if you can hand in your work later.
   b. Not go to class the next day.
   c. Go to class the next day without the homework and say nothing.
   d. Do as much of the work as you can and give it to the teacher the next day.

3 You've got a doctor's appointment and need to leave class early. What would you do?

   a. Not go to class.
   b. Get up and leave the classroom when it's time to go to your appointment.
   c. Explain the situation to the teacher before class.
   d. When it's time to go to your appointment, get up and explain to the teacher why you have to leave.

4 You've got a question about something the teacher has just said in class. What would you do?

   a. Look confused.
   b. Call out, 'I've got a question.'
   c. Raise your hand and ask the teacher to explain.
   d. Wait and ask the teacher to explain after class.

5 You're sitting in the classroom talking to a classmate, when the teacher comes in. What would you do?

   a. Stand up to show your respect for the teacher.
   b. Look up and greet the teacher.
   c. Look down to show your respect for the teacher.
   d. Look up and pay attention to the teacher.

ANSWER KEYS

Task Sheet 1: Social behaviour

1 a. Wrong. 'How are you?' is only a greeting. You should respond by saying something like 'Fine. How are you?' or 'Very well, thanks. And you?' You should not start to talk about your medical problems.
   b. Right.
   c. Right.
   d. Wrong. See answer (a).

2 a. Wrong. It is polite to praise the apartment, but it is impolite to ask how much the rent is.
   b. Right.
   c. Right.
   d. Wrong. You should not walk around the apartment or pick up anything, unless you are invited to do so. You can, however, say something like, 'This is a really nice apartment.'

3 a. Wrong. You should not mention the toilet directly.
   b. Right. Your friend will know what you mean.
   c. Right.
   d. Wrong. You can indicate that you want to use the toilet by saying something like, 'Could I use your bathroom first?'

4 a. Right.
  b. Right.
  c. Wrong. Your friend will probably not ask you again.
  d. Wrong. This would be appropriate only with very, very
  close friends.
5 a. Wrong. Bowing is not a custom in the UK or the US. The
  usual response to an introduction is something like, 'It's nice
  to meet you.'
  b. Wrong. Shaking hands is OK, but you should say
  something. See answer (a).
  c. Right.
  d. Wrong. 'Hi' is a little too informal for an introduction to a
  friend's parents.

Task Sheet 2: Classroom behaviour

1 a. Wrong. This would disrupt the class.
  b. Wrong. You'll miss classwork and could be marked absent.
  c. Wrong. This would disrupt the class.
  d. Right.
2 a. Right.
  b. Wrong. You'll miss classwork and the teacher will probably
  realize why you're absent.
  c. Wrong. The teacher will expect an explanation.
  d. This is OK, but if you do this, you should explain the
  situation to the teacher.
3 a. Wrong. You'll miss classwork and could be marked absent.
  b. Wrong. If you have to leave class early, you should explain
  the situation to the teacher before the class begins.
  c. Right.
  d. Wrong. See answer (b).
4 a. Wrong. The best thing to do is to raise your hand and ask
  the teacher to explain.
  b. Wrong. It's OK to say (but not shout) that you have
  question. But unless there are very few students in the class,
  you should raise your hand to get the teacher's attention.
  c. Right.
  d. This is OK, but it's probably better to ask the teacher to
  explain during class. You're probably not the only student who
  needs an explanation.
5 a. Wrong. Teachers in the UK or the US do not expect
  students to behave so formally.
  b. Right.
  c. Wrong. If you look down, the teacher may interpret this as
  a sign of guilt or lack of interest.
  d. Right.

4.5 Cultural commentary

AIM	Cultural observation and description
MATERIALS	A video travelogue
LEVEL	Upper-intermediate and above
TIME	60 minutes

PREPARATION

1 Find a video travelogue containing typical cultural features, such as folk dancing, a family breakfast, Thanksgiving dinner, etc. Select a descriptive extract of about three minutes.

2 Calculate how many scenes you need to divide the extract into, and time each sequence.

3 Set up the video player and TV monitor in the classroom.

IN CLASS

1 Divide the class into groups of two to four.

2 Explain to the class that they are going to watch a travelogue, but that there is no soundtrack, and that they are going to have to write the script.

3 Play your selected extract once with the sound down. The students meanwhile try to identify the situation.

4 Next, allocate one scene from the extract to each group, who are then to write the commentary for that scene. If you have timed the sequences beforehand, tell the students, so that each group knows how long their commentaries should be.

5 Play the extract with the sound down, pausing at each change of scene as many times as is necessary for the students to take notes. Encourage them to focus on any item that might seem unusual to someone from their culture.

6 The groups write their commentaries for each scene.

7 Play the extract again. This time, each group speaks its commentary. You may wish to record the commentaries on to a cassette recorder and replay it against the video extract.

8 Finally, play the extract with the original sound on. Students compare the cultural points they emphasized with those spoken by the commentator on the video.

REMARKS

Many publishers produce ELT travelogues useful for this type of activity.

Acknowledgement

We are indebted to Michael Rutman in Zurich for this activity.

4.6 Mini-surveys

AIM

To increase awareness of social behaviour and customs in the target culture; to use the target language to interview native speakers, and to prepare and present an oral report

MATERIALS

A questionnaire about customs and social behaviour

LEVEL

Upper-intermediate and above

TIME

60 minutes (over three class sessions, plus extra-curricular time)

PREPARATION

Choose one of the model questionnaires overleaf. Make enough copies to give one to each student. Alternatively, students can make up their own questionnaires.

IN CLASS

Day 1

1 Divide the class into groups of five or six, and distribute the questionnaire.

2 Explain that each group is to interview a cross-section of people who are members of the target culture and then prepare an oral report to present to the class.

3 Groups work together to decide when they will conduct the survey, where they will conduct it, how many people they will interview, and who they will interview.

Day 2

1 When the class meet again, ask the groups to get together to summarize the information they have collected and to prepare an oral report to present to the class. Tell the students that their group reports should include an introduction to the survey, a summary of the results, and a conclusion stating the group's interpretation of the information collected.

2 Groups work together, summarizing the information collected and preparing their oral reports.

Day 3

1 Groups take turns to present their oral reports to the class.

2 After each group has presented its report, allow three to five minutes for the rest of the class to make comments and to ask the group questions.

REMARKS

This activity is obviously most suitable for students studying in the UK or the US. Teachers working in other contexts might consider inviting native-speaker informants and getting the students to interview them in class.

QUESTIONNAIRE

GETTING TO KNOW PEOPLE

Interview four or five native speakers to find out their answers to the following questions. When you do the survey, keep a record of the *yes* and *no* answers, and make notes on any interesting comments that people make.

1 Do you usually wait for the other person to say 'Hello' first?

2 Do you wait for someone to introduce you to someone, rather than introduce yourself?

3 Do you usually re-introduce yourself to people who have forgotten your name?

4 Do you usually smile when you first meet people?

5 Do you usually start conversations with people?

6 Do you usually give short answers, or say only 'Yes' or 'No' to questions?

7 Do you ask for people's opinions, to find out how they think and feel about things?

8 Do you compliment other people on what they say and do?

9 Do you tell people that you would like to get together with them?

10 When you meet people with whom you would like to be friends, do you invite them to an activity or to your home?

QUESTIONNAIRE

ATTITUDES TO TIME AND SPACE

Interview four or five native speakers to find out their answers to the following questions. When you do the survey, note down the individual speakers' answers.

1 When you are invited to someone's house for dinner, how much earlier or later than the scheduled time do you try to arrive?

2 How long does a dinner party usually last?

3 If you were planning a surprise birthday party for a close friend, how many days or weeks in advance would you invite the guests?

4 If you were a guest at a party or at a social occasion in someone's home, how would you indicate to your host that it was time for you to leave?

5 If you had an appointment to meet a friend at 12:00 and arrived at 12:45, how would you expect your friend to react?

QUESTIONNAIRE

INTRODUCTIONS

Interview four or five native speakers to find out their answers to the following questions. When you do the survey, note down the individual speakers' answers.

1 When you are introduced to a man of your age or younger, what do you usually say?

2 When you are introduced to a woman of your age or younger, what do you usually say?

3 When introducing yourself to someone you don't know at a party, what do you usually say?

4 When you are being introduced to someone, do you usually shake hands?

5 What are some topics you might talk about immediately after an introduction?

QUESTIONNAIRE

PERSONAL RELATIONSHIPS

Interview four or five native speakers to find out their answers to the following questions. When you do the survey, keep a record of the *yes* and *no* answers, and make notes on any interesting comments that people make.

1 Do you have close friends from different countries?

2 Do you have friends who are members of other religious groups?

3 Are most of your friends of the same sex as you?

4 Do you prefer going out with a group of friends rather than with one or two friends?

4.7 News photo search

AIM

To deduce information about everyday life in the target culture from news photos

MATERIALS

News photos from a British or American newspaper

LEVEL

Elementary and above

TIME

60 minutes

PREPARATION

Assemble a selection of news photos from a British or American newspaper. (Photos of local or regional news events will usually provide the most relevant information for the discussion points of this activity.) Gather enough photos to give three or four to each group of students.

IN CLASS

1 Divide the class into groups of three or four.

2 Tell the class that you are going to distribute some news photos from a British (or American) newspaper to each group. The groups are to work together, carefully studying each photo and making a list of the features which are different in their home country: hair styles, clothing, architectural styles, urban and rural features, etc.

3 Give each group three or four pictures to look at.

4 Students work together in their groups, looking at the photos and drawing up lists of features. As the groups work together, circulate from group to group, guiding the students to look for relevant information, with questions like:
– *What do you think that building is used for? Does it look like any kind of building in your own country?*
– *Why are those people gathered there?*
– *Why is that man dressed like that? Comment on his clothes.*
– *Look at the car number plate. Is it different from those in your home country? How?*

5 Volunteers take turns, showing the photos to the class and pointing out the culturally-relevant features on their group's list.

VARIATION

Students can be asked to match a group of newspaper photographs with a list of words or expressions (three to five expressions per photograph). For example, if one of the photographs is of a university graduation ceremony, the students would have to match it with the following related vocabulary: *bachelor's degree/sophomore/professor/scholarship.*

4.8 Observation and judgement

AIM   To identify cultural sterotypes through statements and images

MATERIALS   Photographs from magazines

LEVEL   Intermediate and above

TIME   60 minutes

PREPARATION   1 Make up a collection of photographs representing people from a wide variety of cultures in a variety of settings. These can be obtained from newspapers and magazines such as the *National Geographic*. You will need one photograph per student.

2 It may be worth mounting your collection on cards for re-use.

IN CLASS   1 Tell the students that they are going to explore observations about the target culture. Ask them to make a list of five to ten things which they have themselves observed.

2 Write up the following headings and examples on the board:

Observation	*Judgement*
American food isn't very spicy.	*American food is awful.*

Ask the students to differentiate between the two statements. (An observation is something we see, hear, or know to be true. A judgement is a personal opinion on what we see or hear.)

3 Ask the students to think about whether their statements were observations or judgements.

4 Then conduct a whole-class discussion on the following questions:
– *What influences the things we observe?*
– *Why is it important to distinguish between observations and judgements?*
– *How can we improve our observational skills?*
– *Why do we think in cultural stereotypes?*

5 Now pass round the photographs that you have brought to class, giving one to each student.

6 The students work individually, studying and writing five sentences about the picture in front of them. When they have finished writing, they pass what they have written, together with the picture, to another student.

7 The other student marks the sentences O (observation) or J (judgement), and then returns the sentences to the writer.

8 In pairs or in groups, students then discuss why they described the photographs in the way they did.

REMARKS

1 It is extremely important to handle the discussion stage of this activity positively and with delicacy, in order to avoid hurt feelings.

2 The activity may be carried out in two stages, Steps 1–4, and Steps 5–8.

Acknowledgements
This activity is derived from two sources: J. Gaston, 'Cultural orientation in the English as a second language classroom' in D. Batchelder and E. G. Warner (eds.), *Beyond Experience* (Brattleboro, Ver.: The Experiment Press, 1977, pp. 95–6, and H. Ferguson, *Manual for Multicultural Education* (Yarmouth, Maine: Intercultural Press, 1987).

4.9 Social behaviour

AIM

To heighten awareness of the differences in appropriate social behaviour between the students' own culture(s) and that of the UK or the US

MATERIALS

A task sheet for each student

LEVEL

Intermediate and above

TIME

20–30 minutes

PREPARATION

Prepare enough copies of the task sheet below to give one to each student.

IN CLASS

1 Distribute the task sheet to the students.

2 Explain the task to the students. They are to work together in small groups to discuss the situations described on the task sheet, and to decide what would happen in similar situations in their own culture(s).

3 The groups discuss the situations and complete the task sheet.

4 When the groups have finished, lead a short discussion on the situations described, eliciting what would happen in similar situations in the different countries represented by the class. Focus the discussion on the following questions:
– *In which situations is behaviour in the UK or the US different from behaviour in your own country?*
– *In which situations is behaviour similar?*

- *What, if anything, did you learn about behaviour in the UK or the US from this activity?*
- *What, if anything, did you learn about behaviour in your own country?*

Acknowledgement
This activity is an adaptation of one described in an article by Luke Prodromou in the June 1992 issue of *Practical English Teaching.*

TASK SHEET

UK/US	My country
1 When people are invited to a party, they often take a bottle of wine or even bottles of beer.	_____ _____ _____
2 When invited to a dinner party, people usually arrive within fifteen minutes of the appointed time.	_____ _____ _____
3 At an informal party, people don't wait to be introduced. They introduce themselves.	_____ _____ _____
4 When people are being introduced, they try to make direct eye-contact with the other person.	_____ _____ _____
5 After a formal introduction, people often use titles until they are invited to use first names.	_____ _____ _____
6 People shake hands when they meet other people for the first time, but not every time they see them after that.	_____ _____ _____
7 Men and women friends may kiss each other on the cheek if they see each other after a long time, or even each time they meet.	_____ _____ _____
8 People often try to start a conversation with someone they don't know by making a comment about the weather.	_____ _____ _____

9 People may try to start a
   conversation by
   complimenting the other
   person.

10 During the 'farewell' stage of
   a conversation, people will
   often move away from each
   other little by little and
   decrease eye-contact.

4.10 Video observation

AIM

To increase awareness of observable features of the target culture

MATERIALS

A three- to five-minute video sequence illustrating several features of the target culture

LEVEL

Intermediate and above

TIME

30 minutes

PREPARATION

1 Select a sequence from a video containing a variety of cultural features particular to the country or culture involved (for example, a cocktail party scene).

2 Set up the video recorder and monitor in the classroom.

IN CLASS

1 Tell the students that they are going to view a video sequence in which a variety of features particular to the target culture is illustrated. Their task is to watch and make notes on the cultural features they observe.

2 Write four or five questions on the board to guide students towards specific observations. For example, the following questions might be used with a video sequence of a cocktail party:
- *Do people wait to be introduced to each other, or do they introduce themselves?*
- *What kinds of clothes are the people wearing?*
- *How close to each other do the people stand when they are talking?*
- *Do people wait for the host to pour them a drink, or do they help themselves?*
- *What things do people talk about?*

3 Tell the students that you are going to play the video sequence twice. The first time, they are to watch closely. The second time, they are to make notes on the questions, or record other cultural features which they may observe.

4 Play the sequence twice, while the students watch and make notes.

5 After viewing, the students work in groups of three or four, discussing their answers to the questions and any other cultural information they have noted.

6 The students then report back to you. From your knowledge of the culture presented, correct any misconceptions and introduce any additional cultural points you feel are significant. If necessary, play the sequence again.

4.11 What did he do? What did she say?

AIM

To identify culturally appropriate behaviour

MATERIALS

A short video sequence illustrating behavioural features

LEVEL

Lower-intermediate and above

TIME

20–30 minutes

PREPARATION

1 Choose a video sequence which shows an aspect of behaviour in the target culture which is different from that in the students' own culture(s), for example, customs connected with greeting, leave-taking, eating, etc.

2 Set up the video recorder and monitor in the classroom.

IN CLASS

1 Play the sequence once for the students to identify the situation (who the people are, where they are, and what they are doing), and the language (what the people are saying).

2 Tell the students that you are going to play the sequence again, and ask them to focus and make notes on any aspect of behaviour which they find interesting, unusual, or surprising.

3 Play the sequence again. The students observe and make notes.

4 Next, ask the students to say what the people in the sequence said and did. For example, they might say: *A man and a woman met in the street. They hugged each other and kissed each other on both cheeks. The woman said, 'How lovely to see you!'*

5 Discuss the sequence with the class. Ask, for example:
– *What is the situation?*
– *What is the relationship between the people?*
– *What did the people do?*
– *What did they say?*

6 Now ask the students what they would say or do in a similar situation in their culture(s). The students may come up with answers such as: *We would never kiss a man/woman in public. We would never touch someone of the opposite sex.*

7 Try to get the students to explore what lies behind the behaviour. For instance, in the example cited above, kissing on the cheek is more likely to be a sign of affection and courtesy than of immorality! Students from some other cultures may have to make a conscious effort not to be affronted or upset if they see or experience this kind of behaviour.

8 This is a particularly sensitive area. Recommend to your students that, if in doubt, the more traditional and conservative behaviour is the safest. Finally, recommend the behaviour appropriate in the target culture: *If in doubt, shake hands warmly but do not kiss.*

REMARKS

These are some of the major points of behaviour to be aware of:
– Courtesy to women
– Degrees of politeness
– Eating habits
– Greeting
– Kissing, hand-shaking, gestures
– Leave-taking
– Loudness or quietness of the voice
– Seating arrangements in meetings/receptions
– Small talk
– Sniffing/coughing/sneezing/nose blowing, etc.
– Ways of extending invitations
– Ways of giving instructions/orders
– Ways of indicating agreement/disagreement
– Ways of opening/closing meetings
– Ways of beckoning/pointing
– Ways of standing/sitting

5 Examining patterns of communication

The underlying assumption in all the activities in this section is that communication, language, and culture cannot be separated. Successful cross-cultural communication demands cultural fluency as well as linguistic fluency. In order to communicate effectively in English, students need more than just competence in English grammar and vocabulary. They must also have an awareness of the culturally-determined patterns of verbal and non-verbal communication which speakers of English follow (for example, the unwritten rules of speaking—how to begin, continue, and end conversations), the styles of spoken and written language that are most appropriate for particular situations, and the non-verbal communication signals most commonly used in English-speaking cultures.

Culturally different patterns of communication are a common cause of misunderstanding and can be a source of discomfort in cross-cultural situations. For example, a student who comes from a culture in which students are not expected to ask questions or give opinions in class may feel uncomfortable interacting in this way with an American or British teacher. To avoid being misunderstood and to gain self-confidence in interacting in English-speaking situations, students need to develop an understanding of the differences in communication styles between their own and English-speaking cultures.

The activities in this section are designed to increase awareness of native speakers' common expectations of spoken and written communication in English. They also provide opportunities for students to practise the skills needed for successful communication. Some activities, 'Answer, add, and ask' (5.2) and 'Minimal responses' (5.5), focus on particular aspects of conversational style in English. 'Cross-cultural rhetoric' (5.4) heightens awareness of how styles of formal written communication reflect cultural norms.

Activities dealing with non-verbal communication feature strongly in this section. Language classes have traditionally emphasized verbal language. However, non-verbal language, which is closely connected with culture, needs to be dealt with as well. In order to communicate effectively in a culture, it is necessary to be familiar with that culture's non-verbal patterns of communication. For one thing, non-verbal signals acceptable in one culture may be completely unacceptable in another.

Furthermore, studies of the communication of attitudes and emotions in the United States have shown that up to 93 per cent of a message may be transmitted non-verbally. Apparently, the 'body language' we use is at least as important as the words we actually speak. 'Non-verbal signals' (5.7) and 'What's the message?' (5.9) offer suggestions for exploring patterns of non-verbal communication.

Most of the activities in this section can be used effectively in both monolingual and multilingual classes. 'Cross-cultural introductions' (5.3) is most suitable for multilingual classes, although some of the variations will work well in monolingual groups. Similarly, 'Whisperound' (5.10) offers separate suggestions for monolingual and multilingual situations. It goes without saying that the activities focusing on non-verbal communication will be particularly illuminating in classes where a number of different cultural groups are represented.

5.1 Analysing TV conversations

AIM

To increase awareness of common exclamations, fill-in expressions, ways of clarifying meaning, and of initiating, sustaining, and terminating a conversation in English

MATERIALS

A video sequence of a conversation from a TV soap opera; a task sheet for each student

LEVEL

Upper-intermediate and above

TIME

25–30 minutes

PREPARATION

1 Select a brief (five minutes maximum) video sequence from a TV soap opera or serial that provides enough relevant information for students to fill in the task sheet below.

2 Make enough copies of the task sheet to give one to each student.

3 Set up the VCR and monitor in the classroom.

IN CLASS

1 Distribute the task sheet. Tell the students that you are going to play a video sequence of a conversation from a TV show. Their task is to listen and fill in the task sheet with the exclamations and fill-in expressions that the characters use. The students should also note how the characters clarify meaning, and how they begin, continue, and end the conversation.

2 Discuss the task sheet with the students to make sure that they

understand the kind of information required. It may be helpful to write an example of each category on the board:

Exclamation:	*Oh!*
Fill-in expression:	*Er . . ., Uh-huh,* etc.
Clarifying meaning:	*Do you mean . . .?*
Beginning a conversation:	*So, what do you think about . . .?*
Continuing a conversation:	*And then what happened?*
Ending a conversation:	*Well, I've got to go now.*

3 Play the sequence, more than once if necessary.

4 The students work individually, filling in the task sheet.

5 Now ask the students to work in pairs to compare their answers and discuss what they noticed.

6 Ask the students to report back to you. Discuss any interesting points that emerge.

7 Play the sequence once more, so that the students can check their answers.

VARIATION

The students can analyse two or three TV conversations in this way and then compare them.

TASK SHEET

As you watch the video sequence, write down what you hear under the headings below.

Exclamations

_____

Fill-in expressions

_____

Clarifying meaning

_____

Beginning a conversation

_____

Continuing a conversation

_____

Ending a conversation

_____

5.2 Answer, add, and ask

AIM

To heighten awareness of and to practise the reciprocal style of speech common in American and British conversations

MATERIALS

A pencil and pen and a piece of paper for each student

LEVEL

Intermediate and above

TIME

15–20 minutes

PREPARATION

For most classes, no preparation will be needed. However, you may wish to have one or two questions prepared for discussion, in case the students are unable to think of their own, or if you wish to focus discussion on a particular topic.

IN CLASS

1 Explain to the students that in a typical British or American conversation, participants usually practise the three 'A's: 'answer, add, and ask'. In this activity, they are going to have an opportunity to carry on a conversation in the British/American manner. You may wish to read out the following conversation to the class (or write it on the board or overhead transparency). If you write up the conversation, you might want to engage the students from the start in identifying the various stages where each of the three 'A's occurs.

A *Do you think mothers of young children should stay at home and not do a paid job? (Ask)*

B *No, I don't. I don't think all mothers should be expected to stay at home with their children. (Answer) Sometimes mothers have to work outside to support their families. And some fathers might feel happier staying at home with the kids. (Add) What do you think? (Ask)*

A *I agree with you. (Answer) I also feel that businesses should provide childcare for their workers' children. (Add) Why do you think business and industry have been so slow in providing child-care? (Ask)*

B *They probably think it costs too much. (Answer) But the truth is that it's probably good for business. (Add) Don't you agree? (Ask)*

2 Tell students to write down one open-ended question on a controversial issue to ask another student. For example: *How do you feel about couples living together before they are married?* Allow the students two to three minutes to write down their questions.

3 Elicit questions from the students. As they read their questions, write them on the board.

4 Ask the class to vote on the question they wish to discuss.

5 Divide the class into pairs. One student in each pair is A, the other is B. Explain to the students that A will ask B the question. B will answer, add some more information, then ask A

a related question. A will then answer B's question, add some information, ask another related question, and so on.

6 Allow ten minutes or so for the pairs to have their conversations.

7 After the conversations, conduct a whole-class discussion. Focus the discussion on the following questions:
- *How did you feel while doing this activity?*
- *What did you learn about your partner in the conversation?*
- *Is this style of conversation similar to or different from that in your own culture(s)? In what ways is it similar or different?*

5.3 Cross-cultural introductions

AIM	**To practise introductions; to help to develop rapport within a multinational class; to identify members of the class; to learn something about the different cultures represented in the class**
MATERIALS	**No special materials are needed**
LEVEL	**Elementary and above**
TIME	**Variable**
PREPARATION	No special preparation is needed. Note, however, that this activity is best suited to the first meeting of a multinational class in the UK or the US.
IN CLASS	1 Explain the task to the students. They are to introduce themselves to the whole class in their mother tongue, exactly as they would in their own country. When they have done this, they provide a direct translation in English of what they said in their own language. 2 Students take turns to introduce themselves to the class.
VARIATION 1	To increase awareness of how different cultures use different body language to communicate similar meanings, ask the students to introduce themselves non-verbally, using any form they wish.
VARIATION 2	To increase awareness of certain characteristics of the different cultures represented in the class, ask the students to introduce themselves by recounting a significant incident that demonstrates some aspect of their culture.

VARIATION 3   To develop rapport within the class and to reveal some of the students' different expectations about the class, ask them to introduce themselves by telling the class what they hope to gain during the course of the year.

VARIATION 4   To help the other students (and you!) to remember and be able to identify other members of the class, ask the students to introduce themselves by stating one important thing about themselves, in addition to their name.

VARIATION 5   To focus on significant individual characteristics other than names and jobs, ask the students to introduce themselves in any way they wish, as long as they don't mention their names or their jobs.

VARIATION 6   To reveal similarities and differences in the cultural values represented by proverbs, ask the students to introduce themselves by giving a proverb from their country.

VARIATION 7   To help to develop a caring atmosphere within the class, ask each student to introduce a member of the class from another culture after a few minutes' conversation with the other student.

5.4 Cross-cultural rhetoric

AIM   To heighten awareness of specific cultural patterns of interpretation; to compare and contrast different interpretations of different policy statements

MATERIALS   A task sheet for each student

LEVEL   Advanced

TIME   20–30 minutes (unlimited)

PREPARATION   1 Select a paragraph from an institutional publication (for example, a school or university bulletin), in which an official policy involving cross-cultural values is described. Blank out ten to twelve words (see the sample task sheet opposite, and the answer key overleaf).

2 Make enough copies of the task sheet to give one to each student.

IN CLASS   1 Divide the class into groups of three or four, and distribute the task sheet.

2 Explain the task to the students. They are to work in their groups, filling in the blanks on the task sheet with any words they feel are appropriate and meaningful in the context.

3 Allow enough time for the groups to complete the paragraph.

4 Each group then tells the class what they put in each blank, and how they interpreted the paragraph.

5 Read out the original version of the paragraph (or distribute a printed copy of it). The groups compare the original version with their own interpretations.

6 Next, conduct a whole-class discussion on the following questions:
- *In what ways does the paragraph reflect Anglo-American culture?*
- *In what ways does your version of the paragraph reflect your own culture?*
- *How do you feel about the policy described in the original paragraph?*

Acknowledgement
This activity is an adaptation of 'Cross-cultural training exercise for interpreting policy' in W. H. Weeks, P. B. Pedersen, and R. W. Brislin (eds.), *A Manual of Structured Experiences for Cross-Cultural Learning* (Yarmouth, Maine: Intercultural Press, 1979).

SAMPLE TASK SHEET

It is the policy of the University to _____ its members' observance of their major _____ holidays. Where academic scheduling _____ prove unavoidable, no _____ will be penalized for _____ due to _____ reasons, and alternative means will be sought for satisfying the academic _____ involved. If a suitable arrangement cannot be worked out between the _____ and the _____, students and instructors should consult the appropriate department _____ or _____ or the _____ of the College.

ANSWER KEY

> It is the policy of the University to ___*respect*___ its members' observance of their major ___*religious*___ holidays. Where academic scheduling ___*conflicts*___ prove unavoidable, no ___*student*___ will be penalized for ___*absence*___ due to ___*religious*___ reasons, and alternative means will be sought for satisfying the academic ___*requirements*___ involved. If a suitable arrangement cannot be worked out between the ___*student*___ and the ___*instructor*___, students and instructors should consult the appropriate department ___*Dean*___ or ___*Director*___ or the ___*Dean*___ of the College.

5.5 Minimal responses

AIM

To increase awareness of how American and British speakers use questions to show interest in another person; to practise giving answers to questions in a way that will keep the conversation going

MATERIALS

No special materials are needed

LEVEL

Intermediate and above

TIME

10–15 minutes

PREPARATION

Make enough copies of the task sheet opposite to give one to each student.

IN CLASS

1 Tell the students that you are going to read a rather unusual dialogue. Set the scene: *A and B are outside a university classroom. The class is about to begin. A is a British student who is interested in talking to B.*

2 Read the dialogue to the class.

3 When you have read the dialogue, ask the following questions:
– *How does A show interest in B?*
– *Is A likely to remain interested in B?*
– *What is wrong with the conversation?*

4 Once the students understand that B can help the conversation along by asking questions or commenting on what A says, divide the class into pairs, and give a task sheet to each student, and ask them to rewrite and practise the dialogue.

5 Students work in pairs, rewriting and practising the dialogue.

6 When the students have finished, ask for volunteers to read the dialogues to the class.

VARIATION

As an extension of this activity, ask students to make up a list of 'typical questions' that people ask them when they are in the UK or the US (or that an American or British person might ask them in their own country). The students should then try to make up interesting answers to keep the conversation flowing. For example:

A *How do you like the food here?*
B *It's not bad, but I'm used to spicier food. Is there any British food that's spicy?*

TASK SHEET

> Work in pairs. Rewrite the dialogue so that both speakers ask questions. Change the short answers to longer ones, to show that both speakers are interested in the conversation. You may have to change some of the original sentences to fit in with the new ones you add.
>
> A Hello. Are you in this class?
> B Yes.
> A Where are you from?
> B Xanadia.*
> A Did you come to England to study?
> B Yes.
> A What are you studying?
> B Computer science.
> A How long will you be here?
> B Three years.
> A When did you arrive?
> B Last month.
>
> * A fictitious country.

Photocopiable © Oxford University Press

5.6 Multilingual role-plays

AIM

To increase awareness of non-verbal behaviour in English; to highlight some of the differences between non-verbal behaviour in the students' culture(s) and the Anglo-Saxon environment

MATERIALS

No special materials are needed

LEVEL

Lower-intermediate and above

TIME

60 minutes

PREPARATION

No special preparation is needed.

IN CLASS

1 Divide the class into pairs and explain the task to the students. They are to write two versions of a dialogue, first in their own language, then in English. The dialogue may be based on any one of the following situations (list the situations on the board):
– two close friends meeting at a party
– a man and a woman making a date
– a customer returning an article to a salesperson in a shop.

2 Allow fifteen to twenty minutes for the pairs to write their dialogues. Then tell the class that they are to practise their dialogues for a few minutes, so that they can perform them in both versions for the class. Encourage the students to use whatever body language (gestures, facial expressions, eye-contact, etc.) they feel is appropriate in each language.

3 Allow five to ten minutes for the pairs to practise their dialogues.

4 Pairs then take turns to perform their dialogues in front of the class, first in English, then in their own language. After each dialogue, invite the other students to comment on the non-verbal behaviour they observed. Ask questions such as:
– *What differences, if any, did you notice when the languages were changed?*
– *What differences in gestures did you notice?*
– *What differences in facial expressions did you notice?*
– *Were there any differences in eye-contact? If so, what were the differences?*

5 After all the pairs have performed their dialogues, conduct a whole-class discussion on the following questions:
– *What did you learn about non-verbal behaviour in English from this activity?*
– *What did you learn about non-verbal behaviour in your own language?*

REMARKS This activity can work successfully only in classes where it is possible to pair students from the same culture/language community.

5.7 Non-verbal signals

AIM **To increase awareness of and sensitivity to non-verbal communication signals; to practise using non-verbal signals consciously**

MATERIALS **No special materials are needed**

LEVEL **Elementary and above**

TIME **20–25 minutes**

PREPARATION No special preparation is needed

IN CLASS **1** Divide the class into groups of three to four. Ask the students to work together to draw up a list of eight to ten non-verbal signals (for example, a nod, or a wink). Members of each group should demonstrate the signals they think of, not describe them in words. You might like to demonstrate one or two non-verbal signals to the students to get them started.

2 The students work in their groups, demonstrating and listing their signals.

3 When all the groups are ready, students take turns to demonstrate a non-verbal signal. The rest of the class try to guess the meaning of each signal.

VARIATION **1** As a follow-up or alternative, students can play a version of charades.

2 Make up a list of eight to ten simple sentences such as the following, and write each one on a card:
– *There's a bug on the wall!*
– *I feel cold.*
– *Get out of here!*
– *Answer the telephone.*
– *The floor is hot.*
– *This is delicious.*
– *Come in, please.*
– *Your baby is beautiful!*
– *This tastes terrible.*
– *I'm angry!*

3 Divide the class into two teams, A and B. One member of team A chooses a card and acts the sentence non-verbally. The other team A members have to try to work out the meaning, while someone times them. Next, team B have to work out a sentence chosen and acted out by one of their own team. The team with the lowest time-score wins.

5.8 Role playing emotions

AIM	**To increase awareness of how particular emotions are expressed non-verbally in different cultures; to review the vocabulary of emotions**
MATERIALS	**No special materials are needed**
LEVEL	**Intermediate and above**
TIME	**Variable**
PREPARATION	No special preparation is needed.
IN CLASS	1 Write a list of eight to ten words indicating different emotions on the board. For example:

happiness	joy
sadness	pain
fear	nervousness
guilt	courage

Make sure that the students understand the words on the list.

2 Arrange the class so that the students are seated in a circle and can all see one another. If there are more than twenty people in the class, divide the class into two or more groups, each group seated in a circle.

3 Tell the students that within their groups they are to take turns to choose one of the emotions listed on the board and mime it for the group. They may use facial expressions and body language to express the emotion, but no words or sounds.

4 Students take turns to act the emotions. Group members try to guess the emotion being played.

5 Follow up with a whole-class discussion focusing on the following questions:
- *Which emotions are expressed similarly by different cultures?*

- *Which emotions are expressed differently?*
- *What have you learned about cross-cultural communication from this activity?*

5.9 What's the message?

AIM	**To discover the meaning of some common gestures in English**
MATERIALS	**A hand-out for each student**
LEVEL	**Intermediate and above**
TIME	**15–20 minutes**
PREPARATION	Make enough copies of the hand-out below to give one to each student.

IN CLASS

1 Ask the students to work in pairs. Distribute the hand-out and write the following questions on the board:
- *What does each gesture mean?*
- *Which ones could you use in the UK or the US?*

2 Students work together, discussing the gestures on the hand-out and answering the questions.

3 Each pair takes it in turn to report their interpretations to the class.

4 After all the pairs have finished, point out to the class which gestures would be understood by speakers of English. If necessary, clarify the meanings.

VARIATION 1

As an extension to this activity, ask the students to discuss the following questions:
- *Which of the gestures, if any, are different from the gestures used in your culture?*
- *In what situations do you use gestures?*
- *Are there any gestures you should not use with certain people?*

VARIATION 2

In multilingual classes, ask the students to demonstrate some gestures that are common in their country to see if other members of the class can guess the meanings.

SAMPLE
HAND-OUT

The gestures that would be understood by speakers of English are: 1, 2, 3, 4, 5, 6, 8, 9 (American), 11, and 12.

Number 1 means 'Good luck!' or 'I hope everything goes well!'

Number 2 means that a person is crazy. It is often used as a joke and is normally used only when talking privately about a third person.

Number 3 means 'I don't know' or 'I have no idea'.

Number 4 means 'I can't/didn't hear you'.

Number 5 means 'That's enough' or 'It's all over for me'.

Number 6 is the 'thumbs down' sign, used to indicate rejection or refusal.

Number 7 is used in some parts of the world to mean 'Something's a bit suspicious/odd here'.

Number 8 means 'Come here'.

Number 9 is widely used in the US (but not in Britain, where a 'thumbs up' sign is used) to mean 'OK'.

Number 10 is used in Italy to say 'Hello'. For Indonesians, Malaysians, and some speakers of Arabic, it signals 'Come here'. Some speakers of English might confuse this gesture with the wave for 'Goodbye'.

Number 11 means 'Oh, I forgot' or is used as an expression of surprise.

Number 12 means 'Slow down', 'Relax', or 'Wait a second'.

Gestures not used in the UK or US are numbers 7 and 10.

Acknowledgement

This activity is an adaptation of 'The message is . . .' in Rob Nolasco and Lois Arthur, *Conversation* (Oxford University Press, 1987), pp 64–5.

5.10 Whisperound

To increase awareness of the difficulty of translating meaning accurately to another language

No special materials are needed

Upper-intermediate and above

15–20 minutes

(This activity is designed for classes in which the students all speak the same native language. For multilingual classes, see the variation below.) No special preparation is needed.

1 Ask for six student volunteers. The volunteers should seat themselves in a circle.

2 Explain the procedure to the class. You are going to whisper a rumour in English to the first person in each circle. That person will translate the rumour and whisper it in the native language to the second person. The second person will translate the rumour back into English and whisper it to the next person, and so on. The last person in the circle will translate the rumour into English and tell it to the class.

3 Whisper a fairly complicated three- or four-sentence rumour (about some topic of interest to the class) to the first person in the circle. An example of the kind of rumour might be: *Did you know that a Martian spaceship landed in Australia this morning and kidnapped fifty kangaroos? And that they then went off to the moon to set up a kangaroo colony?*

4 The other students in the class act as observers, while the rumour is being transmitted around the circle.

5 Volunteers take turns to tell the class the difficulties they encountered in translating the rumour.

VARIATION

This exercise can still be effective and illuminating in multilingual classes, where the transmission of the rumour is done entirely in English. In the follow-up discussion, students can be asked to imagine what would happen if the rumour whisperound took place in two or more languages. Focus the discussion on the following questions:
– *What difficulties, if any, would you have in translating the rumour into your own language?*
– *What additional differences might there be between the original and the final versions of the rumour?*
– *What does this activity suggest about the difficulty of translating meaning from one language to another?*

Acknowledgement
This activity is an adaptation of a technique described in 'Rumour transmission using multiple translations' in W. H. Weeks, P. B. Pedersen, and R. W. Brislin (eds.), *A Manual of Structured Experiences for Cross-Cultural Learning* (Yarmouth, Maine: Intercultural Press, 1979), pp. 13–14.

6 Exploring values and attitudes

One way of defining a culture is by the implicit cultural assumptions it makes: the values, beliefs, and attitudes which lie so deep within a culture that they are seldom, if ever, questioned. Most often they are taken as 'givens' which any educated, intelligent person *anywhere* would accept. Needless to say, not every educated, intelligent individual *everywhere* shares all of the values and attitudes of English-speaking cultures. Many, perhaps most, of the world's people adhere to systems of values and attitudes that are radically different from those held by people from English-speaking cultures. The major goal of this section is to increase students' consciousness of cultural differences in values and attitudes: to help students to become more aware, not only of the assumptions of English-speaking cultures, but of their own culturally influenced assumptions, and of the diversity of ideas and practices found across cultures in general.

Because values and attitudes are so often taken for granted, this section places strong emphasis on activities which encourage students to recognize and explore their own cultural assumptions, including their preconceptions and stereotypes about both the target culture and other cultures. Examples of activities which fall into this category include 'Examining stereotypes' (6.5) and 'Superior attitudes' (6.9). Examples of activities which focus on increasing awareness of the values and attitudes of English-speaking cultures are: 'Commerical values' (6.2) and 'Lost and found' (6.6). 'Agree or disagree?' (6.1) and 'Connotations' (6.3) share the goal of stimulating recognition and discussion of the diversity of values and attitudes which will be represented by any class, whether all the students come from the same culture or not.

All of the activities in this section are suitable for either monolingual or multilingual classes. 'Stereotypes I have heard' (6.8) and 'The people speak' (6.10) are most suitable for classes of students living and studying in the target culture.

6.1 Agree or disagree?

AIM

To stimulate discussion of cultural values and attitudes; to practise reaching consensus; to practise rewording sentences

MATERIALS

A task sheet for each student

LEVEL

Intermediate and above

TIME

25–30 minutes

PREPARATION

Make enough copies of the task sheet below to give one to each student. Alternatively, you may wish to make up your own controversial sentences.

IN CLASS

1 Distribute the task sheet to the students (or write the sentences on the board).

2 Explain the task to the students. They are to read each statement and indicate whether they agree or disagree with it.

3 The students work through each statement on the task sheet.

4 Divide the class into groups of three or four. Tell the students they are to discuss each statement with their group. If *anyone* disagrees with a statement, the group changes the wording in such a way that *everyone* in the group agrees with it.

5 The groups discuss and modify the statements.

6 Ask each group to report on one or two statements. Then ask other groups for their alternative versions.

REMARKS

Since the opinions expressed may be intensely personal, this activity should not be done with a recently-formed class. The technique of sentence modification can be adapted and used with any social issue likely to be of interest to the students, for example, marriage, the roles of women and men, etc. The advantage of the technique lies not so much in the validity or otherwise of the statements, but in the discussion they stimulate.

TASK SHEET

Read the following statements. Indicate whether you agree or disagree with them.

1 Foreigners who go to live in a new country should give up their foreign habits and adapt to the new country as soon as possible.

2 Many of the world's populations do not take enough initiatives to develop, so they stay underdeveloped.

3 English should be accepted as the universal language of the world.

> 4 Some of the world's populations have not yet reached the higher stages of civilization.
>
> 5 Minority members of any population should conform to the customs and values of the majority.

Acknowledgement
This activity is adapted from Robert Kohls, 'Reaching consensus' in *Intercultural Sourcebook: Cross-Cultural Training Methodologies*, D. S. Hoopes and P. Ventura (eds.) (La Grange Park, Il.: Intercultural Network Inc., 1979), p. 60.

6.2 Commercial values

AIM

To increase awareness of some of the cultural values reflected in British and/or American TV commercials; to compare and contrast these with the students' cultural values

MATERIALS

A video recording of a British and/or American TV commercial; a task sheet for each student

LEVEL

Upper-intermediate and above

TIME

25–30 minutes

PREPARATION

1 Choose a UK/US TV commercial which provides enough relevant information and discussion points for this activity. Record the commercial on videotape.

2 Make enough copies of the task sheet below to give one to each student.

3 Set up the VCR and monitor in the classroom.

IN CLASS

1 Give each student a copy of the task sheet. Tell the class that the list on the task sheet identifies certain cultural values that can influence people's behaviour. Make sure that the students understand each item in the list.

2 Tell the students that you are going to play a British (or American) TV commercial. The students' task is to think about the values on the list as they watch each commercial, and put a tick (✓) in the boxes next to the values they see reflected in the commercial.

3 Play the commercial two or three times.

4 The students work individually on the task sheet.

5 Divide the class into groups of three or four. Within the groups, the students compare their answers and discuss the observations they made about the commercial.

6 Groups take turns to report their observations to the class.

7 Play the commercial once more, so that the students can confirm or modify their responses to it.

8 Finally, conduct a whole-class discussion on the following questions:
– *Are TV commercials common in your country?*
– *If so, what products, services, etc., do they advertise?*
– *How are commercials in your country similar to the one you have just seen?*
– *How are they different?*

VARIATION 1

You could bring in several commercials on video and ask the students to analyse them in the same way, and then compare them.

VARIATION 2

Ask the students to write the commercial as they would expect to see it in their own culture, or as they would like to see it.

TASK SHEET

Which of the following values do you think are reflected in the commercial you have just seen? Tick (√) the boxes.

☐ Fast, busy pace of life
☐ Concern with 'doing' (action), progress, change
☐ Optimism
☐ Material objects
☐ Spiritual goals
☐ Self-reliance, individual responsibility
☐ Good health
☐ Comfort
☐ Competition
☐ Respect for authority
☐ Planning for the future
☐ Informality
☐ Friendship with both sexes
☐ Friendship with same sex only
☐ Youth, vigour

6.3 Connotations

AIM   To associate vocabulary learning with cultural contexts

MATERIALS   Vocabulary items

LEVEL   Lower-intermediate and above

TIME   15 minutes

PREPARATION   Choose ten words which the students have already learned. If possible, ask a native speaker to record the words and write down one or two words which he or she associates with them.

IN CLASS   1 Write the ten words on the board (for example, *tea, police, church, dinner, home, right, blue, breakfast, sport, animal*).

2 For this activity, students may use dictionaries if they wish. The students work individually, writing down a word they associate with each word on the board. For example: *Breakfast—croissant/cheese/fish/rice.*

3 Now ask the students to work in pairs. The students then compare their lists with each other.

4 Pairs take turns to report back to the class. Write up the students' new words next to the appropriate word on the board. Make sure that the class understand the new words.

5 Discuss with the class which words are personal and which words reflect the students' culture(s).

6 Next explain to the class that you are going to write up on the board the associations made by a speaker of English.

7 Conduct a whole-class discussion on the following questions:
– *What are the differences between the native speaker's associations and those of the students?*
– *What, if anything, do the differences say about the native speaker's culture?*

Word	Associations
Breakfast	*croissant/cheese/fish/rice/salad* (students) *toast/porridge/eggs* (native English speaker)

Acknowledgement
This is based on an activity devised by Simon Greenall.

6.4 Encounter

AIM

To increase awareness of cultural stereotypes; to extend the vocabulary of description

MATERIALS

A short video sequence showing someone in an interesting setting, or a large photograph of a person

LEVEL

Intermediate and above

TIME

10–15 minutes

PREPARATION

1 Choose a photograph or a video sequence showing someone you know well, surrounded by people and things, either in a room or outside. There should be enough detail for the class to be able to make assumptions about the person.

2 If you intend to use video, set up the VCR and monitor in the classroom.

IN CLASS

1 Explain to the class that you are going to show them a photograph (or a video sequence) of a person. They are to study the person for one minute.

2 Show the photograph or video. The students observe and think about the person.

3 Divide the class into groups of three or four. Ask the groups to discuss the video/photograph and to draw some conclusions about the person, under the following categories:
– *Name*
– *Age*
– *Occupation*
– *Kind of family*
– *Background*

4 Write the categories up on the board.

5 When the groups are ready, ask them to report back to the class everything they feel they 'learned' about the person, giving reasons for their assumptions.

6 Next, tell the class who the person is, and anything about his/her background that is not confidential.

7 Then conduct a whole-class discussion on the following questions:
– *What differences were there between what you observed and the 'real' facts?*
– *What features of the video/photograph led you to different conclusions?*

6.5 Examining stereotypes

AIM

To examine the stereotypes held by the students in the class; to explore how and why they originated; to recognize that they are often invalid and lead to misunderstanding

MATERIALS

No special materials are needed

LEVEL

Intermediate and above

TIME

30 minutes

PREPARATION

(This activity is most suited to multilingual classes living and studying in the target culture.) No special preparation is needed.

IN CLASS

1 Elicit the names of all the countries represented by the students in the class, and write them on the board. When you have finished, tell the students that you are going to say each of the names in turn.

2 Ask the students to write down the names of the countries on a piece of paper as you say them, and then write down the first three things they think of when each country is mentioned. It is important that the students do *not* write their own names on the papers.

3 Collect the students' papers and read out the names of the countries and what was said about each one.

4 Ask individual students to react to what was written about their countries. For example, you might say: '*Gue Nam, how do you feel about what was written about Korea?* Try to avoid making your own comments. Simply let the students give their own reactions to what was written.

5 Follow up with a whole-class discussion on the following questions:
– *Without saying exactly what you wrote, why did you write the things you did?*
– *Where did your ideas about the different countries come from?*
– *Have your ideas about people from different countries changed since you have been here? If so, in what way?*
– *Why are some stereotypes harmful?*
(They don't allow for individuality, they encourage negative judgement, and lead to misunderstanding.)

6.6 Lost and found

AIM

To find out what kinds of thing British/American people place value on; to practise deducing factual information from newspaper advertisements

MATERIALS

A number of 'Lost and Found' advertisements from British and/or American newspapers

LEVEL

Elementary and above

TIME

60 minutes

PREPARATION

Collect a variety of 'Lost and Found' advertisements from a British or American newspaper. Make sure that you have enough to give each student a complete set of advertisements.

EXAMPLES

UK

COLLEGE SCARF Wool navy/white stripes, 4ft long (St Hilda's College, Oxford). In pub on Osney Island last Saturday. Small reward. Please ring 792070 evening.

CAT Large British standard domestic tabby (neutered tom) with white socks, answers to 'Derby', vegetarian. Probably homesick. If found, please phone 724441. Reward.

NAME BRACELET Silver chain-link engraved Allergic to penicillin. Lost this week in Hampstead area. Urgent find quickly. Phone 071 435 7746 for reward.

£20 NOTE dropped in Little Clarendon Street on Saturday. 2% reward. Ring 56868.

DOG small golden brown collie-type female found on river barge, Park End Street. Ring 243087 daytime.

RING oval cut diamond in white gold 4 prong setting, 48 points. Reward. 081 960 3428 evenings only.

CARDIGAN hand-knitted fine purple wool. Found on park bench University Parks. Ring 247958.

BOOK Copy of The Prophet lost at weekend in countryside near Worminghall. Please return if found. Huge sentimental value. Small reward. 339348.

TOOLBOX high quality tools found in blue toolbox in baker's shop last Friday. Call Woodruffs for information.

US

CAT black. 30 April at 1846 Bishop's Ferry Road. Wearing red collar. $50 reward. 956 2345.

DIAMOND RING (Ladies') Lost at Baltimore aquarium. Reward. Call 301 266 9684.

NEW BOXED ELECTRIC TOASTER French make (tefal) Found on road Sunday. 633 8640.

KEYS (SET) Lost Monday Peachtree/Lake area. Call 962 3684.

SCHNAUZER silver male, name Gustav. Van Ness/Reno area Brown collar. Reward. 362 4259.

SIGNET RING GA Tech, near Milton and Sandell Drive. Reward 404 553 8126 after 5 p.m.

DOG small med-brown short haired female. Found near Oakdale Rd S. 691 0532.

ENVELOPE Sealed, pale blue, 8in by 4in, marked AG. Great sentimental value. Please return for reward. (212) 382 3800.

SALUGI puppy, fine golden short hair. Found Georgetown University campus Friday. Call 262 8638.

TENNIS BRACELET in or around Clayton stadium. Reward. 633 1924

IN CLASS

1 Ask the students if they have ever lost or found anything valuable. What kinds of thing did they lose or find? As the students name the items, write them up on the board.

2 After the students have mentioned as many things as they can, distribute the advertisements and explain the task to the students. They are to read the advertisements and make a list of the different things the advertisers have lost or found.

3 The students work individually, making their lists.

4 After the students have finished, ask for volunteers to name the different things that people have lost and found. Write the names of the things on the board.

5 Write the following questions on the board:
– *Are 'Lost and Found' advertisements common in your country?*
– *If so, what sorts of thing are usually mentioned in the advertisements?*
– *How are the British/American advertisements similar to 'Lost and Found' advertisements in your country?*
– *How are they different?*

6 Divide the class into groups of three or four. The students work in groups, discussing the questions.

7 Follow up with a whole-class discussion on the following questions:
– *Why do people go to the trouble and expense of placing an advertisement in a newspaper for something they have lost?*
– *What did you learn from this activity about the things that British/American people place value on (both financial and non-financial)?*

VARIATION 1

Instead of analysing 'Lost and Found' advertisements, ask the students to examine the advertisements in the 'Personal' columns. Focus the discussion on the following question:
– *For what kinds of reason do people advertise in the 'Personal' columns?*

VARIATION 2

Alternatively, you might ask the students to analyse announcements of births, marriages, and deaths. Ask the students to discuss these questions:
– *In what ways do the announcements differ from similar announcements in your own country?*
– *What attitudes towards death (or birth or marriage) can you deduce from reading the advertisements?*
– *In what ways, if any, are the advertisements similar to those in your own country?*

REMARKS

Almost any type of newspaper advertisement can be used to deduce facts about daily life and to gather information about the values of the target culture. For other activities using advertisements, see 'Help wanted' (3.5), 'Housing available' (3.7), and 'What would you like to do?' (3.12).

6.7 Proverbial values

AIM

To discover cultural values through proverbs

MATERIALS

A task sheet with a list of proverbs in English

LEVEL

Advanced

TIME

30–40 minutes

PREPARATION

Make enough copies of the task sheet below to give one to each student. Alternatively, you may wish to draw up your own list of proverbs and make up a task sheet.

IN CLASS

1 Introduce the topic of proverbs, and give a task sheet to each student.

2 Explain the task to the students. They are to work individually, reading the proverbs and writing down the value which they think each proverb teaches.

3 Allow the students enough time to complete their task sheets.

4 When the students have finished, divide the class into groups of three or four.

5 The groups work together, comparing and discussing their answers.

6 Each group then reports to the class on the values they perceive in each proverb.

VARIATION 1

At the lower levels, you can give the students a list of values to match with the proverbs (for example, *adaptability*, *generosity*, *health*, *optimism* (×2), *persistence*, *precaution* (×2), *privacy*, *promptness* (×2), *thrift*.

VARIATION 2

Another way to extend this activity is to ask the students to write down any other proverbs they know in English, and to explore the values that the proverbs express.

VARIATION 3

You can also ask the students to make up lists of proverbs from their own culture(s) and then present their lists (and the values expressed through them) to the class. Students can compare and contrast the values expressed with the values expressed in English-language proverbs.

REMARKS

The items on the task sheet represent a few fairly random examples of proverbs in English. The essential point of the activity, that basic values are expressed by proverbs, can be made with a dozen or so proverbs or axioms from any culture.

Acknowledgement
This activity is an adaptation of 'Discovering American values through American proverbs' in L. R. Kohls, *Developing Intercultural Awareness* (Washington, D.C.: Society of Intercultural Education, Training, and Research, 1981).

ASK SHEET

Here are some proverbs often used in English-speaking countries. Next to each proverb, write the cultural value that you think the proverb teaches. The first one has been done for you.

Proverbs

Values

1 A penny saved is a penny earned.

Economy or thrift

2 A stitch in time saves nine.

_____

3 Good fences make good neighbours.

_____

4 There's no time like the present.

_____

5 It's better to give than to receive.

_____

6 An apple a day keeps the doctor away.

_____

7 When in Rome, do as the Romans do.

_____

8 Every cloud has a silver lining.

_____

9 Rome wasn't built in a day.

_____

10 Make hay while the sun shines.

_____

11 You're never too old to learn.

_____

12 Look before you leap.

_____

6.8 Stereotypes I have heard

AIM

To examine stereotypes and preconceived ideas held about th target culture; to recognize how and why they are formed; to realize that some of the stereotypes may be invalid and can lead to misunderstanding

MATERIALS

A task sheet for each student

LEVEL

Intermediate and above

TIME

60+ minutes in two class periods (plus extra-curricular time)

PREPARATION

(This activity is best suited to students living and studying in th UK or the US.) Make copies of a task sheet similar to the one opposite for each student.

IN CLASS

Day 1

1 Write the word *stereotype* on the board and ask the students to give you an example of one. If the students have difficulty in finding one, you may wish to suggest one, for example: *All Americans are rich.* Then ask the students to try to explain the difference between a stereotype and a generalization. (A stereotype does not allow for individuality, and often encourages critical or negative judgement. A generalization, for example: *There are some very wealthy people in the United States*, is non-judgemental and allows for individuality.)

2 Distribute the task sheet. Tell the students to use the left-han column to list five stereotypes they have heard about people in the UK (or the US, depending on where the students are). In th middle column they are to indicate whether they personally believe that the stereotype is true or not, and give reasons for their answers. The right-hand column will be filled in later with reactions given by native speakers of English to be interviewed by the students.

3 Allow enough time for the students to fill in the left and middle columns on the task sheet.

4 For homework, ask the students to interview at least three people from the target culture to see how the interviewees react to the stereotypes listed. The students should then fill in the right-hand column with the interviewees' reactions, and note any interesting comments.

Day 2

1 When the class meet again, ask each student to read out one c two of the stereotypes, together with the interviewees' reactions.

2 Conduct a whole-class discussion on the following questions:
- *Which stereotypes were most frequently mentioned?*
- *Where do these ideas come from?*
- *Have any of your ideas about this country changed since you came here?*
- *What have you learned from this activity?*

TASK SHEET

Stereotypes	In your opinion, is it true? Why/Why not?	Answers of people from the country stereotyped
1		

6.9 Superior attitudes

AIM

To increase awareness of ethnocentric language and attitudes; to stimulate discussion of ethnocentrism; to provide opportunities for students to express their views; to practise rewording statements to make them less ethnocentric

MATERIALS

A task sheet for each student

LEVEL

Intermediate and above

TIME

15–20 minutes

PREPARATION

Make enough copies of the task sheet below to give one to each student.

IN CLASS

1 Write the following sentence on the board: *People in my country are much friendlier than people in your country.*

2 Ask for volunteers to say how they feel when someone makes such a statement. After several students have spoken, tell the class that the sentence is an example of an *ethnocentric* attitude. It suggests that one country or culture is superior to others. (You may wish to write the word *ethnocentric* on the board.)

3 Explain the tasks to the students. Tell them that they are going to complete two tasks on the task sheet. Task A is to identify the ethnocentric attitudes in the sentences. Task B is for the groups to change some of the statements so that they are no longer ethnocentric.

4 Divide the class into groups of three or four, and distribute the task sheet.

5 The students complete tasks A and B, discussing the answers in groups.

6 When everyone has finished, ask each group to report their reactions and revisions of one or two of the statements.

Acknowledgement
This activity is adapted from an activity in D. R. Levine and M. B. Adelman, *Beyond Language: Intercultural Communication for English as a Second Language* (Englewood Cliffs, N.J.: Prentice Hall Regents, 1982).

TASK SHEET

Task A
Read the following statements and underline the words or phrases that express an *ethnocentric attitude* (the attitude that one race, nationality, religion, or culture is superior).

1 Mentonia has produced the finest works of art in the world.
2 Mentonia is a superior country because it has produced the greatest technology in the world.
3 Non-Mentonians do everything the wrong way round.
4 The Mentonian language is the best language for poetry.
5 The Mentonian people have been very generous in teaching people in other countries how to do things the right way.
6 If everyone did things the Mentonian way, the world would be a better place.

Task B
With your partners, choose one or two of the statements above and change the wording so that the statements are no longer ethnocentric. For example:
Ethnocentric statement: *Mentonia has produced the world's greatest literature.*
Revised statement: *Mentonia has many writers who have produced well-known works of literature.*

6.10 The people speak

AIM

To become aware of the attitudes of target-language speakers; to practise reading, speaking, and writing a summary

MATERIALS

A newspaper or magazine article about a controversial situation or event in the target culture

LEVEL

Intermediate and above

TIME

60+ minutes, in two class periods (plus extra-curricular time)

PREPARATION

(This activity is most suitable for students living and studying in the target culture.) Choose a short newspaper or magazine article dealing with a controversial situation or event in the target culture (for example, homelessness). Make sure that you have enough copies of the article to give one to each student.

N CLASS

Day 1

1 Distribute the article and allow the students enough time to read it. Clarify any questions they have about vocabulary, etc.

2 Conduct a whole-class discussion on the following questions:
– *What did you learn from the article?*
– *What are your feelings about the situation or event?*

3 Next, ask the students to formulate a question which will elicit an opinion from a target-culture interviewee. For example, if the article is about homelessness in American cities, the question might be:
– *What do you personally think should be done about homeless people in American cities?*

4 Explain the task to the students. They are to use the question to interview eight to ten people from the target culture. They then summarize their findings in a one-page written report to present to the class. Set the date for the reports to be made.

Day 2

1 Students take turns to read their reports to the class.

2 Conduct a whole-class discussion on the following questions:
– *Was there any consistency in people's answers to the question?*
– *What, if anything, surprised you about people's answers to the question?*
– *What did you learn from this activity?*

6.11 'Trap' words

IM

To identify words and phrases containing a mismatch between linguistic meaning and cultural connotation

MATERIALS

Words and expressions from textbooks and articles

EVEL

Intermediate and above

IME

10 minutes

PREPARATION

1 Choose ten words and phrases which may have cultural connotations different from their purely linguistic meaning. For example:

– *How are you?* (This is a polite formula, not a request for information about a person's health.)

– *Of course.* (This simply means *It's obvious*, and has nothing to do with the course of things.)

– *Let's have lunch some time.* (This is not always an invitation. More often it is a way of disengaging from a conversation.)

– *Buon appetito/bon appétit/guten Appetit!* (There is no equivalent for this expression in English, quite simply because we do not say anything to people about to start their meal.)

– *Please.* (Introduces a polite request. It does not relate to *pleasing*.)

– *Pardon?* (This means, *Could you please repeat what you said?* It is *not* asking for forgiveness!)

– *Sorry.* (Although this is an apology, it need not indicate deep, heartfelt regret.)

– *Excuse me.* (Is not asking for leniency. It is just a way of attracting attention.)

– *Sir/Madam* (These rather formal titles are used in special situations.)

– *Have a nice day!* (This cheerful farewell, used commonly in the US, may be considered insincere in Britain.)

2 Write or type the words or phrases you have chosen, and mount them on cards for later re-use. You may wish to make up your own list of 'trap' words.

IN CLASS

1 Divide the class into pairs or small groups.

2 Give each pair or group a card with one of the words or phrases on it. Explain to the students that they are to make up a dialogue, using the word or phrase on their card.

3 While the students are making up their dialogues, circulate around the class, offering help if requested.

4 Each pair or group rehearses the dialogue among themselves.

5 Next, the groups present their dialogues to the class.

6 When all the groups have finished, conduct a whole-class discussion on the following questions:

– *In each case, was the word or phrase used in the right way, and in the right context?*

– *What were the problems you experienced in trying to get it right?*

– *To what extent, if any, did your own language and cultural habits affect the task?*

– *What did you learn from this activity?*

7 After the discussion, ask each pair or group to revise their dialogue so as to correct the cultural context.

Acknowledgement
This is adapted from an activity devised by Simon Greenall.

6.12 Values clarification: global problems

IM
To heighten awareness of global issues; to begin to clarify one's own values with respect to global issues; to practise giving reasons for and proposing solutions to global problems

ATERIALS
No special materials are needed

EVEL
Intermediate and above

ME
30 minutes

REPARATION
Write the following table on the board:

	Problem	Reason	Solution
1	_____	_____	_____
2	_____	_____	_____
3	_____	_____	_____
4	_____	_____	_____
5	_____	_____	_____
6	_____	_____	_____
7	_____	_____	_____
8	_____	_____	_____
9	_____	_____	_____
10	_____	_____	_____

CLASS
1 Ask for volunteers to name some problems of a global nature that they are concerned about, for example, poverty, AIDS, global warming, destruction of rain forests and the ozone layer, etc. Elicit ten such problems and write them on the board.

2 Divide the class into groups of three or four, and ask the groups to copy the grid on the board onto a piece of paper.

3 When the groups have finished, explain the task. The groups are to work together and use the grid to rank the problems from 1 to 10, in order of seriousness or urgency (1 being the most serious or urgent problem, and 10 the least serious or urgent problem.) They should list at least one reason for each of their choices.

4 The students work in groups, ranking the problems and listing reasons for their choices.

5 Ask the students to continue working in their groups and to suggest solutions to the most important problems. It may be helpful to elicit one or two sample solutions. (For example, provide more jobs, increase spending on medical research, control pollution more effectively, ban logging, etc.) before the students go on to complete the grid with their own solutions.

6 Groups report their ranking of the problems, the reasons for their choices, and their suggested solutions.

Acknowledgement
This activity is an adaptation of one described in an article by Luke Prodromou in the June 1992 issue of *Practical English Teaching*.

6.13 Word associations

AIM	**To develop awareness of the influence of culture on one's values; to reveal various perceptions of the native and target cultures**
MATERIALS	**No special materials are needed**
LEVEL	**Intermediate and above**
TIME	**Variable**
PREPARATION	(This activity is suitable for monolingual or multilingual classes. No special preparation is needed.
IN CLASS	**1** Divide the class into groups of five or six, and ask each group to arrange themselves so that they are seated in a circle.

2 Ask the students to write down the first five words that come to mind when the name of their home country (or home town) is mentioned.

3 The students take turns to read their words to their group and explain why they chose those words.

4 Repeat Steps 2 and 3, this time using the target culture as the focus.

5 When the students have finished, conduct a whole-class discussion on the following questions:
– *What did you learn about your own cultural values from this activity?*
– *What did you learn about the target culture's values?*

7 Exploring and extending cultural experiences

The final chapter of this book comprises a series of activities designed to allow students to discuss and draw conclusions from their own experience of the target culture, either directly or as a result of what they have heard or read.

One of the key activities in this section is 'Intercultural crisis' (7.5), which arose from the need of teachers in Japan to find ways of calming the very real concern of Japanese college students over the shooting of a Japanese exchange student in the United States. This activity is designed to offer a framework for discussing issues which threaten harmony and good relations between peoples of different cultures.

'Question wheel' (7.7) is a simple activity which allows students to share their experiences of the target language and the target culture. 'Cultural identity' (7.1) allows students to consider their own cultural identification more deeply and to analyse their experience of the target culture.

'Culture flowchart' (7.2) and 'Just a (cultural) minute' (7.6) are entertaining ways of getting students to summarize and revise their knowledge of cultural topics, while 'Culture mini-lectures' (7.3) offers a useful technique to the teacher who needs to present a substantial amount of cultural information in a more formal way.

Cross-cultural exchange is a crucial part of building cultural awareness. Two of the activities in this section offer ways of achieving this. 'Real interviews' (7.8) is a way of using community resources by inviting native speakers to visit your class, and 'Curriculum links' (7.4) offers ideas on how to link up with schools in the target-culture country. This activity also shows how training in cultural awareness need not be linked to language alone, but can extend to the exchange of information on content subjects across the curriculum.

7.1 Cultural identity

AIM

To increase awareness and stimulate discussion of cultural influences and experiences that influence cultural identity

MATERIALS

A task sheet for each student

LEVEL

Advanced and above

TIME

60 minutes

PREPARATION

Make enough copies of the task sheet below to give one to each student.

IN CLASS

1 Introduce the topic of cultural identity. You could say something like: *We are all products of something we call culture. Today we are going to discuss how our cultural background and other experiences influence our cultural identity.*

2 Distribute the task sheet. Tell the students to work individually and to write down their answers to the questions.

TASK SHEET

1 When asked to describe yourself, do you think of yourself as belonging to a particular nationality, religious, or ethnic group? If so, which ones, and why?

2 What experiences have you had that increased your sense of belonging to a particular group?

3 How has your own background influenced:
   a. the way you spend your holidays?
   b. the way you express yourself, verbally and non-verbally?
   c. the way you think about and relate to other groups?
   d. the way you choose your friends?

4 What experiences have you had with people from cultural backgrounds different from your own?
   a. friendships
   b. social relationships
   c. work relationships
   d. travel contacts
   e. media exposure (films, TV, etc.)

5 Have you ever experienced any communication problem because of differences between your own and another person's cultural background?

6 What can individuals do to make communication between themselves and people of other cultural backgrounds more effective?

Explain that the class will discuss the questions when everyone has finished.

3 When all the students have finished, use the questions as the basis for a whole-class discussion. If you have a very large class, you may wish to divide the class into smaller groups for the discussion.

7.2 Culture flowchart

AIM

To establish the sequence of events in a cultural process; revision of process vocabulary

MATERIALS

No special materials are needed

LEVEL

Intermediate and above

TIME

30 minutes

PREPARATION

1 Choose a topic that can usefully be studied in flowchart form, for example, buying a house, finding a job, or going to school. List the points that you want to include in the flowchart, and write each one on a separate piece of paper. It is worth mounting these on cards for re-use.

2 Make enough sets of the flowchart items to give a complete set to each group of five students.

3 Draw a sample flowchart on another topic (such as the sample flowchart at the end of this activity) on the board, to show the class how a flowchart works.

IN CLASS

1 Tell the students what topic they are going to study. Discuss the value of flowcharts, and explain to the students that they are going to create a flowchart of their own from the items you give them.

2 Divide the class into groups of five.

3 Give each group a complete set of the flowchart-item cards.

4 Ask the groups to put them in the right order.

5 When all the groups have finished, ask each group to report to the class on the order that they chose, and to give reasons for their ordering.

6 Discuss any discrepancies in the ordering.

7 Each group then designs a flowchart on the basis of the items.

8 The most accurate/most useful could be put on the class notice-board.

**SAMPLE
FLOWCHART**

The possible courses of Mary's education (Britain)

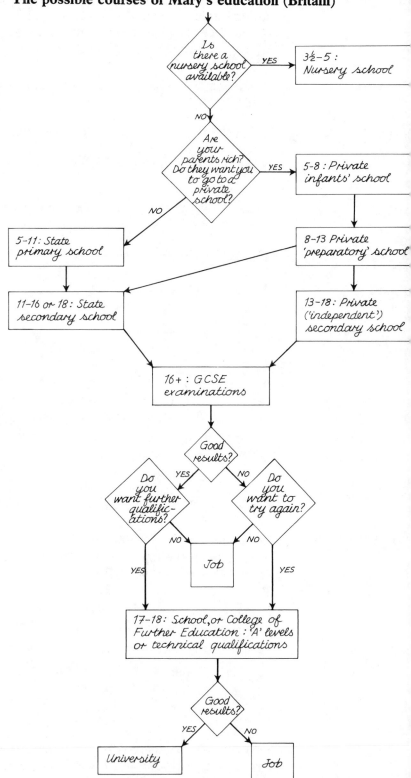

REMARKS

1 Flowcharts are an effective way of fixing in the mind processes and the order in which things happen (for example, the passing of a law, or progress through the education system). They work even more effectively if they are produced by the students themselves.

2 The example opposite shows a simplified version of the British education system.

VARIATION

Instead of putting items on cards, write the items in random order on the board. An experienced class can generate their own flowcharts from the beginning.

7.3 Culture mini-lectures

AIM

Comprehension checking; feedback

MATERIALS

No special materials are needed

LEVEL

Intermediate

TIME

20 minutes

PREPARATION

This is a technique for the teacher who has to give a lecture to the class about a particular aspect of culture. Before the class, divide the substance of the lecture into segments lasting one and a half or two minutes.

IN CLASS

1 Introduce the topic to the class.

2 Explain that you will talk on some aspect of the topic for two minutes. The students will then have to summarize what you said in their own words.

3 Talk about the topic for two minutes, then stop and ask the students to tell you what you have just said.

4 The students summarize what you said. If the students have any difficulty, ask prompt questions to help them. For example: *How many newspapers are there?*

5 Correct any misunderstanding or misinterpretation (but not language), and then carry on for another two minutes. In this way you can check step by step that the class know how to listen sensitively and have understood your presentation.

6 You may wish to tell the class about the next presentation, for example: *Future parts of this mini-lecture will cover: owners owning more than one newspaper; the difference between daily and Sunday newspapers; magazines in Britain. A later mini-lecture may be about the media (radio and TV).*

VARIATION

An extension of this activity is to ask the students to prepare their own mini-lectures on culture and deliver them to the class.

SAMPLE LECTURE

Today let's look at the British Press. The word 'press' describes newspapers and magazines. We use the word 'media' to describe radio, TV, and satellite broadcasting. The British read a lot of newspapers. Some families take two newspapers every day. We make a distinction between two types of newspapers—quality and popular. Popular newspapers present the news in a more entertaining fashion and do not go into so much detail. An example is the *Daily Express*. Quality newspapers present the news in a lot of detail and are more difficult and take longer to read. An example is *The Times*.

*Now, tell me what I've said about British newspapers so far. (If you need to elicit information, ask questions such as: *What's the difference between press and media? Do the British read newspapers? What's the difference between the two types of newspapers mentioned?*)

Now listen again. One of the words you'll hear a lot is 'tabloid'. One of the big differences between the popular and quality press is the way papers are presented. The popular papers often have a smaller page size, called 'tabloid'. They also tend to have larger headlines (these are the titles of the articles), and more pictures. The quality newspapers have fewer pictures, smaller headlines, and longer articles. They also have a larger page size. The technical word for them is 'broadsheet', but you do not hear this much in everyday speech.

However, the real reason why the word 'tabloid' is so common is because part of the tabloid press has a particular approach to the news—especially the *Sun* and the *Daily Mirror*. They are the newspapers that report royal scandal in every detail—partly out of 'public interest' and partly out of a desire to sell more newspapers! When people refer to 'the tabloids', they are often referring to these newspapers, rather than the *Daily Mail* or the *Daily Express*. *Now tell me what I have just said.

Now listen again. The main quality daily newspapers are: *The Times*, the *Financial Times*, the *Daily Telegraph*, the *Guardian*, and the *Independent*. These are all distributed nationally, but there are also important regional daily newspapers, such as the *Glasgow Herald* in Scotland. The main tabloid popular newspapers are the *Sun*, the *Daily Mirror*, the *Daily Star*, the *Daily Express*, and the *Daily Mail*. An important word in relation to newspapers is 'circulation'. 'Circulation' describes the number of copies sold every day. The best-selling newspaper in Britain is the *Sun*, with an average daily circulation of about 4,000,000 copies. The best-selling quality newspaper is *The Times*. This sells only 500,000 every day.

An important question in the British Press is who owns
newspapers. British newspapers are owned by private individuals,
and to some extent the politics of the newspaper reflects the
politics of the owner. The socialist party in Britain (the Labour
party) believes that the press mainly supports the Conservative
party. Only one newspaper, the *Daily Mirror*, officially supports
Labour.
* Now tell me what I have just said.

7.4 Curriculum links

AIM

**To link teaching about English language and culture to
curricula in other countries; to create links between schools in
the target-culture country**

LEVEL

Intermediate and above

TIME

Variable and on-going

PREPARATION

This activity is most suitable for classes outside the target culture
who wish to have close contact with a class or classes of native
speakers of English.

1 You will need to establish contact with a teacher in an English-
speaking school, either directly through colleagues or between
the education authorities in your country and those of the target-
culture country. In Europe, one way of doing this is to promote
school links in the context of town twinning.

2 When the link is established, agree with the contact teacher in
the linked school about areas of the curriculum on which
information can be exchanged.

3 Agree also how the information is to be exchanged, and
whether it should be by fax, telephone, computer modem, or
teleconference, etc.

IN CLASS

1 The first step is to present the concept of curriculum links to
your students. Explain that in exchanging information, they will
have to decide how they wish to present themselves, and what
they would like to know about the students in their twinned
school.

2 Divide the class into working groups of five or six. Explain
that each group is to list the kind of information about the
school, themselves, their own curriculum, and their lives that
they wish to share with the twinned school.

3 When the groups have completed their lists, they report to the class. The groups try to reach a consensus on the information to be shared. Representatives from each group then join up to write the information to send to the twinned school.

4 The next stage of the project is to ask the groups to formulate the information which the class would like from the twinned school. They then send their questions to the school.

5 When information arrives from the twinned school, the class studies it and answers any questions. Establish a fax link or make a telephone call to clarify any outstanding queries.

6 Your class can also exchange lists of key curriculum projects in subjects other than language (for example, in geography, history, and any other content subject about which information can be exchanged).

VARIATION 1

Devise a project of interest to your students, and which involves obtaining and writing up information from the other school. When the class has all the information and has completed the project, the students send a copy of it to the twinned school.

VARIATION 2

If contact with a school in the target-culture country is impossible, it may be possible to set up links with an English-medium school such as an International School in your country.

REMARKS

1 The success of these exchanges depends on a regular link between the teachers involved, and a commitment to exchanging information quickly and at the agreed times.

2 Access to a telephone and fax, if available, is an important factor in the success of communication.

7.5 Intercultural crisis

AIM

To help students to understand and overcome resentment over incidents that may cause cultural disharmony

MATERIALS

Newspaper articles describing a troubled cultural incident, or a video sequence showing such an incident

LEVEL

Intermediate and above

TIME

60+ minutes on two days (plus extra-curricular time)

PREPARATION

1 Try to collect press reports of an incident that caused cultural disharmony between two different cultural groups. Ideally you should have reports in both English and the learners' mother tongue. Also collect news reports from TV, eyewitness accounts, face-to-face interviews, and 'Letters to the Editor'. Divide up the 'facts' articles from the 'opinions' articles, or highlight the 'opinion' sentences in articles which are a mixture of fact and opinion. Cut them out so that they can be pinned on the classroom wall. Find photos or radio/video interviews with the main protagonists. These can be used to study character and motivation.

2 If you are going to use a video sequence, set up the VCR and monitor in the classroom.

N CLASS

Day 1

1 Tell the class that this activity will consist of eight sections. The class will explore and reach conclusions in the eight areas. Write the following on the board:
– *What have you heard?*
– *How do you feel?*
– *What actually happened?*
– *What are people's opinions?*
– *What are the people like?*
– *Analysis*
– *Action*

2 Ask the class what they have heard or read about the incident. The students describe what they have heard, and write down a few sentences describing the incident.

3 Next, ask the students how they feel about the incident. They choose words to describe their feelings. As they say the words, write them up on the board and discuss them with the students.

4 When they have finished describing their feelings, tell the class that you are going to put up the articles you have collected on the wall.

5 Divide the class into groups of five or six. Each group in turn goes to the wall and removes one article. The group reads the article and notes down just the facts of what happened.

6 When they are ready, each group goes to talk with another group to check their facts against information gathered from a different source by the other group and to try to build an accurate sequence of events together.

7 Tell the students that before the next class they should try tactfully to get as many personal opinions as they can from people outside the class, to find out how people feel about the incident.

Day 2

1 Ask the students to work in groups again to talk about the opinions they heard, and to discuss which opinions they agree with.

2 Next, use the photographs and radio and TV interviews you have collected to give the class an idea of the personalities of the main protagonists. Ask the students to look for information that might give a clue to the protagonist's motivation for causing the incident.

3 In trying to analyse the incident and people's reactions to it, ask the students to focus on the following questions:
- *What does the incident tell you about the other community's culture?*
- *What does the incident tell you about your own culture?*
- *What do you feel you have learned from this activity?*

4 If the students feel very strongly that some action is needed, they could propose, for example, writing a petition, or a letter to a newspaper, to an embassy, or to an organization such as Amnesty International.

5 If you have a video recorder, the students may wish to make a video expressing their views.

7.6 Just a (cultural) minute

AIM

To improve oral composition and fluency and the ability to discuss a cultural topic

MATERIALS

No special materials are needed

LEVEL

Intermediate and above

TIME

15 minutes

PREPARATION

No special preparation is needed, but bring a stop watch to class if you have one.

IN CLASS

1 Explain the activity to the class. You are going to give them a cultural topic, and one person at a time will have to talk on that topic for one minute. If the person speaking hesitates, another person may pick up the topic and continue. Whoever is speaking at the end of the minute gets two points.

2 Divide the class into two, three, or four teams.

3 Give the topic to the first team. Explain that the other teams can challenge on the grounds of hesitation or inaccuracy.

4 Start the stop watch. A member of the first team begins. If he or she is challenged, stop the stop watch.

5 If the challenge is valid, a member of the challenging team continues. If the challenge is inaccurate, the challenging team loses a point.

6 At the end of the activity, the team with the most points wins.

REMARKS

This activity can be used for revision of cultural topics previously studied in class. Such topics might include:
- The American/British Press
- The United States Congress
- UK and US pop music
- A typical day at a British school
- The rules of cricket/softball
- Education in America
- Typical British food
- Famous black Americans
- Northern Ireland, Scotland, Wales, and England

7.7 Question wheel

AIM

To stimulate discussion of cultural experiences and issues

MATERIALS

A large cardboard circle, divided into quarters, with a movable dial in the middle

LEVEL

Elementary and above

TIME

30 minutes

PREPARATION

Prepare a large cardboard circle (about 18 inches in diameter), divided into quarters. Pierce the centre of the circle with a dial that will spin. In each quarter, write a question focusing on the students' contact with or knowledge of the target culture. The result should look like this:

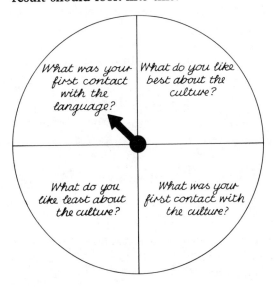

IN CLASS

1 Explain to the class that they are going to play a game. Each student in turn will spin the dial. When the dial stops, the student who spun the dial will answer the question that the dial is pointing to.

2 After each student has answered a question, invite the other students to comment on his or her answer.

3 After all the students have had a chance to spin the dial once, they can spin again for another question.

VARIATION

Students can make up the questions to write on the circle.

7.8 Real interviews

AIM

To talk to native speakers of the target language; to improve questioning techniques; to practise listening and interviewing skills

MATERIALS

No special materials are needed

LEVEL

Intermediate

TIME

20–30 minutes

PREPARATION

1 Identify a native speaker unknown to the class and invite him/her to visit the class. It is important that the class should not know about it in advance.

2 Brief the visitor, so that he/she knows to answer questions normally but not volunteer any extra information.

3 Bring a stop watch to class if you have one.

IN CLASS

1 Invite the visitor into the class and seat him/her at the front.

2 Explain the task to the students. They have three minutes in which to find out as much as they can about the visitor.

3 Ask the students to start the interview. If they have difficulty getting started, you can help them with questions such as: *Ask if he/she is married. Ask about his/her job.*

4 As soon as the students start, time the interview and give them exactly three minutes.

5 At the end of the three minutes, ask the class to tell the visitor what they have learned.

6 Ask the visitor to provide feedback on the accuracy and quantity of information that the class have gathered.

7 The visitor is now free to go. Discuss the interview again with the students. Ask them to think of any additional questions they might have asked, especially follow-up questions.

VARIATION

As an extension to this activity, you could ask the same visitor to come to your class again to give the students practice in asking follow-up questions.

REMARKS

This is an effective way of motivating students as a warm-up to the presentation of cultural material. This activity also ensures that the students learn to listen and improve their understanding of the material you present.

Bibliography

Textbooks for students

Adams, T. W. 1987. *Body English: A Study of Gestures.* Glenview, Il.: Scott, Foresman, and Company.

Archer, C. M. 1991. *Living with Strangers in the U.S.A.: Communicating Beyond Culture.* Englewood Cliffs, N.J.: Prentice Hall Regents.

Ford, C. K. and **A. M. Silverman.** 1981. *American Cultural Encounters.* San Francisco: Alemany Press.

Genzel, R. B. and **M. G. Cummings.** 1986. *Culturally Speaking: A Conversation and Culture Text for Learners of English.* New York: Harper and Row.

Jackson, R. M. and **R. J. Di Pietro.** 1992. *American Voices: An Integrated Skills Reader.* Boston: Heinle & Heinle.

Kearny, E. N., M. A. Kearny, and **J. Crandall.** 1984. *The American Way: An Introduction to American Culture.* Englewood Cliffs, N.J.: Prentice Hall Regents.

Levine, D. R. and **M. B. Adelman.** 1982. *Beyond Language: Intercultural Communication for English as a Second Language.* Englewood Cliffs, N.J.: Prentice Hall Regents.

Levine, D. R., J. Baxter, and **P. McNulty.** 1987. *The Culture Puzzle: Cross-Cultural Communication for English as a Second Language.* Englewood Cliffs, N.J.: Prentice Hall Regents.

McPartland, P. 1983. *Americana: A Basic Reader.* New York: Harcourt Brace Jovanovich.

Mejia, E. A., M. Kennedy-Xiao, and **L. Pasternak.** 1992. *American Picture Show: A Cultural Reader.* Englewood Cliffs, N.J.: Prentice Hall Regents.

Stevenson, D. K. 1987. *American Life and Institutions.* Stuttgart: Ernst Klett Verlag. (Reprinted 1989 by the Bureau of Educational and Cultural Affairs, United States Information Agency.)

Vaughan-Rees, M. 1991. *The London Book.* London: Macmillan.

Videos for teaching cultural awareness

About Britain. 1988. London: Macmillan.

American Culture in Modern Contexts. 1986. Orem, Utah: Producers Consortium.

BBC Essential English Guide to Britain. 1990. London: BBC English.

Cold Water: Intercultural Adjustment and Values Conflict of Foreign Students and Scholars at an American University. 1988. Yarmouth, Maine: Intercultural Press.

Cross Talk: Multi-racial Britain. 1982. London: National Centre for Industrial Training.

Going International: Beyond Culture Shock. 1983. San Francisco: Copeland Griggs.

Going International: Bridging the Culture Gap. 1983. San Francisco: Copeland Griggs.

Going International: Living in the U.S.A. 1986. San Francisco: Copeland Griggs.

People and Places: British Life and Culture for Students of English. 1990. London: BBC English.

When Cultures Meet Face to Face. 1986. Penfield Associates. (Distributed by Dr Eileen Hansen, 155 Mill Road, Edison, N.J. 08818, USA.)

Sources cited and background reading for teachers

Batchelder, D. and **E. G. Warner** (eds.). 1977. *Beyond Experience: The Experiential Approach to Cross-cultural Education.* Brattleboro, Ver.: Experiment Press and Society for Intercultural Education, Training, and Research.

Brislin, R., K. Cushner, C. Cherrie, and **M. Yong.** 1986. *Intercultural Interactions: A Practical Guide.* Sage Publications.

Coben, S. and **L. Ratner** (eds.). 1983. *The Development of an American Culture.* Second edition. New York: St Martin's Press.

Condon, J. C. and **F. Yousef.** 1975. *An Introduction to Intercultural Communication.* New York: Macmillan.

Damen, L. 1987. *Culture Learning: The Fifth Dimension in the Language Classroom.* Reading, Mass.: Addison-Wesley.

Ferguson, H. 1987. *Manual for Multicultural Education.* Yarmouth, Maine: Intercultural Press.

Gaston, J. 1977. 'Cultural orientation in the English as a second language classroom' in D. Batchelder and E. G. Warner (eds.), *Beyond Experience: The Experiential Approach to Cross-cultural Education.* Brattleboro, Ver.: Experiment Press and Society for Intercultural Education, Training, and Research, pp. 95–6.

Hall, E. T. 1976. *Beyond Culture.* New York: Anchor Press/Doubleday.

Hall, E. T. 1966. *The Hidden Dimension.* New York: Doubleday.

Hall, E. T. 1961. *The Silent Language.* New York: Fawcett.

Hall, E. T. and **M. R. Hall.** 1981. *Understanding Cultural Differences: Germans, French and Americans.* Yarmouth, Maine: Intercultural Press.

Holmes, H. and **S. Guild.** 1979. 'Culture assimilators' in D. S. Hoopes and P. Ventura (eds.), pp. 77–91.

Hoopes, D. S. and **P. Ventura** (eds.). 1979. *Intercultural Sourcebook: Cross-cultural Training Methodologies.* LaGrange, Il.: Intercultural Network, Inc.

Kohls, L. R. 1981. *Developing Intercultural Awareness.* Washington, D.C.: Society for Intercultural Education, Training, and Research.

Landis, D. and **R. W. Brislin** (eds.). 1982–3. *Handbook of Intercultural Training: Vols. I–III.* New York: Pergamon.

Lanier, A. R. 1988. *Living in the U.S.A.* (Fourth Edition). Chicago: Intercultural Press.

Luedtke, L. S. (ed.). 1991. *Making America: The Society and Culture of the United States.* Washington, D.C.: United States Information Agency.

Murphey, T. 1992. *Music and Song.* Oxford: Oxford University Press.

Nolasco, R. and **L. Arthur.** 1987. *Conversation.* Oxford: Oxford University Press.

Penfield, J. 1987. *The Media: Catalysts for Communicative Language Learning.* Reading, Mass.: Addison-Wesley.

Prodromou, L. 1992. 'From cultural background to cultural foreground'. *Practical English Teaching*, June, pp. 27–8.

Reese, J. W. 1968. 'Stamp detectives—using postage stamps in social studies'. *Grade Teacher*, October, pp. 113–14.

Robinson, G. L. N. 1985. *Crosscultural Understanding.* New York: Prentice Hall.

Seelye, H. N. 1988. *Teaching Culture.* Lincolnwood, Il.: National Textbook Company.

Smith, G. and G. Otero. 1977, revised 1988. *Teaching About Cultural Awareness.* Denver, Col.: Center for Teaching International Relations.

Stewart, E. C. 1972. *American Cultural Patterns: A Cross-cultural Perspective.* Yarmouth, Maine: Intercultural Press.

Thiagarajan, S. and **B. Steinwachs.** 1990. *Barnga: A Simulation Game on Cultural Clashes.* Yarmouth, Maine: Intercultural Press.

Valdes, J. M. (ed.). 1986. *Culture Bound: Bridging the Cultural Gap in Language Teaching.* Cambridge: Cambridge University Press.

Walsh, J. E. 1979. *Humanistic Cultural Learning: An Introduction.* The University Press of Hawaii.

Weeks, W. H., P. B. Pedersen, and **R. W. Brislin** (eds.). 1979. *A Manual of Structured Experiences for Cross-cultural Learning.* Yarmouth, Maine: Intercultural Press.

Appendix

Sources of cultural information

US

The United States Information Service (USIS) operates more than 150 resource centres around the world. For information about the nearest USIS resource centre to you, contact the US embassy in your capital city.

The United States Travel and Tourism Administration also has offices in several countries. For information, or to find out if there is an office near you, write to:

US Travel and Tourism Administration
14th Street and Constitution Avenue N.W.
Washington
DC 20230
USA

or contact the US embassy in your capital city.

The US Postal Service Philatelic Sales Branch sells mint US stamps. Its address is:

US Postal Service
Philatelic Sales Branch
Kansas City
MO 64144-9998
USA
Tel: (816) 455 0790.

UK

The British Council has offices in 90 countries. Many have libraries and resource centres. For the address of your nearest British Council office, contact:

The British Council
10 Spring Gardens
London
SW1A 2BN
UK
Tel: (071) 930 8466.

The British Tourist Authority has 32 offices worldwide. For the address of your nearest office, contact:

British Tourist Authority
Thames Tower
Black's Road
Hammersmith
London
W6 9EL
UK

The Royal Mail Philatelic Bureau sells mint British stamps. The address is:

British Philatelic Bureau
20 Brandon Street
Edinburgh
EH3 5TT
UK
Tel: (031) 550 8900.

Language focus index

Other titles in the Resource Books for Teachers series

Beginners, by Peter Grundy—provides over 100 original and communicative activities for teaching both absolute and 'false' beginners. Includes a section aimed at learners who do not know the Latin alphabet. (ISBN 0 19 437200 6)

CALL, by David Hardisty and Scott Windeatt—offers the teacher a bank of practical activities, based on communicative methodology, which make use of a variety of computer programs. (ISBN 0 19 437105 0)

Class Readers, by Jean Greenwood—practical advice and activities to develop extensive and intensive reading skills, listening activities, oral tasks, and both perceptive and literary skills. (ISBN 0 19 437103 4)

Classroom Dynamics, by Jill Hadfield—a practical book to help teachers maintain a good working relationship with their classes, and so promote effective learning. It contains activities for ice-breaking and fostering self-confidence, as well as a chapter on 'coping with crisis'. (ISBN 0 19 437096 8)

Drama, by Charlyn Wessels—first-hand, practical advice on how to use drama to promote language acquisition, to improve coursebook presentation, to teach spoken communication skills and literature, and to make language learning more creative and enjoyable. (ISBN 0 19 437097 6)

Grammar Dictation, by Ruth Wajnryb—also known as 'dictogloss', this technique improves students' understanding and use of grammar. By reconstructing texts, students find out more about how English works. (ISBN 0 19 437097 6)

Learner-based Teaching, by Colin Campbell and Hanna Kryszewska—contains over 70 language practice activities which unlock the wealth of knowledge that learners bring to the classroom. (ISBN 0 19 437163 8)

Literature, by Alan Maley and Alan Duff—an innovatory book on using literature for language practice. The activities can be used not only with the sample materials provided, but with materials of the teacher's own choice. (ISBN 0 19 437094 1)

Music and Song, by Tim Murphey—ideas for using all types of music and song in the classroom in lively and interesting ways. It shows teachers how 'tuning in' to their students' musical tastes can increase motivation and tap a rich vein of resources. (ISBN 0 19 437055 0)

Newspapers, by Peter Grundy—full of creative and original ideas for making effective use of newspapers in lessons. The activities are practical, need little teacher preparation, and can be applied to a wide range of articles and extracts. (ISBN 0 19 437192 6)

Project Work, by Diana L. Fried-Booth—provides practical resources for teachers who are interested in bridging the gap between the classroom and the outside world by integrating language learning with projects. (ISBN 0 19 437092 5)

Role Play, by Gillian Porter Ladousse—an ideal vehicle for developing fluency and integrating the four skills. Activities range from highly controlled conversations to improvised drama, and from simple dialogues to complex scenarios. (ISBN 0 19 437095 X)

Self-Access, by Susan Sheerin—is designed to help EFL and ESL teachers with the practicalities of setting up and managing self-access study facilities and so enable learning to continue independently of teaching. (ISBN 0 19 437099 2)

Translation, by Alan Duff—explores the role of translation in language learning and provides teachers with a wide variety of translation activities from many different subject areas. No specialist knowledge or previous experience of translation is required. (ISBN 0 19 437104 2)

Video, by Richard Cooper, Mike Lavery, and Mario Rinvolucri—a practical book which encourages students to explore the interaction between camera and image, and provides them with real tasks involving the language of perception, observation, and argumentation. (ISBN 0 19 437192 6)

Vocabulary, by John Morgan and Mario Rinvolucri—offers a wide variety of communicative activities for teaching new words to learners of any foreign language, by encouraging personal responses and facilitating exploration and extension of the language. (ISBN 437091 7)

Writing, by Tricia Hedge—and award-winning book which presents a wide range of writing tasks to improve learners' 'authoring' and 'crafting' skills, as well as guidance on student difficulties with writing. (ISBN 0 19 437098 4)

Young Learners, by Sarah Phillips—ideas and materials for a wide variety of language practice activities, including arts and crafts, drama, games, storytelling, poems, and songs. The book also gives guidance to teachers new to teaching English to young learners. (ISBN 0 19 437195 6)